FACING ADVERSITY WITH GRACE

LESSONS FROM THE SAINTS

Woodeene Koenig-Bricker

Published by The Word Among Us Press
7115 Guilford Road
Frederick, Maryland 21704
www.wau.org

19 18 17 16 15   3 4 5 6 7
ISBN: 978-1-59325-160-4
eISBN: 978-1-59325-437-7

Cover design by Christopher Tobias

Library of Congress Cataloging-in-Publication Data

Koenig-Bricker, Woodeene.
 Facing adversity with grace : lessons from the saints / Woodeene
Koenig-Bricker.
    p. cm.
 ISBN 978-1-59325-160-4
 1. Christian saints--Biography. 2. Suffering—Religious aspects—
Catholic Church I. Title.
 BX4655.3.K64 2012
 282.092'2--dc23
 [B]
                                    2012009779

Facing Adversity with Grace

Lessons from the Saints

TABLE OF CONTENTS

INTRODUCTION

I've long been intrigued by the lives of the saints. One of my earliest memories is reading *A Picture Book of Saints* (I think it's still on a shelf in my library). However, even as a child, I must have been a bit of a skeptic because I can remember thinking that many of the stories sounded like fairy tales. In particular, Simeon Stylites (ca. 390–459 A.D.), who lived on the top of a tower for thirty-nine years, sparked my incredulity. Just how did he go to the bathroom? I'd been camping often enough to know that all the possibilities I could imagine didn't bode well for anyone unlucky enough to be standing under his tower. Clearly, the lives of the saints were missing some important details!

When I became an adult, I realized that when it comes to saints, biography and hagiography aren't the same—not by a long shot. Biography is the historical recollection of an individual's life, while hagiography—literally "holy writing"—is the specialized form of biography that deals with saints, and saints only. Unlike biographers who want to get to the truth of a life, no matter how scandalous, hagiographers often want to ensure that their subjects are portrayed as truly deserving of sanctity, so anything unbecoming or unseemly (unless it is gloriously redeemed) is glossed over, and, in fact, actual events are sometimes "massaged" a bit to fit the overarching pious message.

This came home to me on the day that Mother Teresa of Kolcata died. Her doctor, who was being interviewed on television, said that her last words were "I can't breathe," something perfectly reasonable for a person who is dying of congestive heart failure.[1] However, it is now widely reported that she said, "I love you, Jesus." Of course it's possible that she said both things and that her Indian doctor, being more in tune with the medical aspects than with Christian prayer, only remembered and reported the part that had to do with the cause of her death. But I'm also pretty sure that anyone wanting to guarantee that she be remembered as holy and eventually canonized wasn't going to have her talking about lack of breath in her last statement. A biographer would want to know what she actually said; a hagiographer wants us to remember what she said that contributed to her sanctity. If this sort of discrepancy can happen in the twentieth century, imagine what might have been remembered about earlier saints. It's not surprising that some of them appear to have had no real human characteristics at all!

That's why, in all my writing about the saints, I've tried to take St. Thérèse of Lisieux's words to heart: "We should not say improbable things, or things we do not know [about the saints]. We must see their real, and not their imagined lives." I've always tried to find out the real story behind the legends, not what people might have wanted the saints to be, say, or do, say.

In *Facing Adversity with Grace*, I've taken a few liberties with what the saints might have been thinking because I've had to tease out lessons from their lives. But I've done my best not to credit those I've written about with "improbable things," nor to create fantasy stories out of whole cloth and pious desire. Because of that, you might not find some of your favorite saints or most cherished stories here. My criterion has been simple: If the reports of a saint raise my eyebrows and sound "too good to be true," I tend to think they may have been dressed up a bit with pious imagining and holy hopes.

One other thing about the saints: I believe that some of them may have walked the tightrope between holiness and madness. (Maybe coming that close to the face of the Divine does that to you. I don't know since I'm not in any danger of canonization!) However, that's the reason you won't find much talk of saints in this book who appeared to take pleasure in suffering for suffering's sake or who induced suffering by extensive self-punishment. If a saint's approach to suffering would not be considered emotionally healthy today, I haven't included it as a contemporary lesson.

That doesn't mean that I don't appreciate people like Rose of Lima, my own patron saint, who destroyed her beauty by tossing lye on her face. I understand that the saints who did such things were doing what they believed God wanted in the context of the spiritual practices of their time and place. However, if I don't find their way of approaching suffering to be very helpful for my own life, I assume that you, the reader, probably won't either.

The saints in this book, even though they come from a variety of eras and cultures, are men and women who can teach us how to live with adversity and the inevitable pain that comes from being human. They also show us how to cope with some of the more common types of adversity today—from financial stress to family issues to struggling with addictions or weight. It is adversity that most of us will be familiar with in one degree or another. I have included questions for your reflection at the end of each chapter as well as a prayer, often from the saint.

My goal here is not to glorify pain, nor is it to make anyone feel guilty if he or she isn't as enthusiastic about suffering as some of the saints seemed to be. I firmly and absolutely believe (as I will discuss in the first chapter) that God does not want us to suffer but wants us to live abundant lives. While we all will experience some pain on our life journeys, becoming entrenched in suffering is not honoring God, nor is it living abundantly. So my hope for you is that as you read how the saints faced suffering and adversity, you will discover not just words of spiritual consolation but genuine, practical measures for your daily life in order to eliminate unnecessary pain and to claim the abundant life that God has promised each one of us. After all, this life in the "vale of tears" may not always be easy, but it is always good!

Woodeene Koenig-Bricker

Chapter 1

Adversity and God's Love

When I was growing up, I believed that God loved adversity and the suffering that comes with it. I erroneously assumed that God thought our pain was the best gift that we could give him and that he wanted everyone to suffer—as much as possible and as often as possible. I'm not quite sure where I got that idea. Perhaps I reasoned that if Jesus' suffering on the cross had made God happy, then my own suffering would also make him happy and that he would love me more as a result. I do know that the sisters in my grade school were very fond of telling stories about the incredible adversities of the saints, always making sure we got the underlying point that we should be emulating them if we wanted to go to heaven.

Since I was a very earnest and pious child, I did my utmost to fulfill what I believed was this obligatory path to holiness. I performed many acts of penance in my quest to suffer for the love of God. For instance, when I was eight years old, I gave up all my recesses and lunch hours during Lent so that I could pray the Rosary in church, even though I did not enjoy praying the Rosary. (Don't be shocked—I still don't, and neither did St. Thérèse of Lisieux, who found it sleep inducing.) Over the years I denied myself many legitimate and even worthwhile activities, thinking that somehow my suffering was making God love me more. I looked for ways to make myself miserable, believing that there was a direct correlation between my unhappiness and

God's approval and love. I even took the name Rose, after St. Rose of Lima, for my Confirmation because I was fascinated by the fact that she destroyed her beauty in the name of holiness. (Looking back, I realize that I was a bit of a morbid child!)

That pattern continued well into my adult life. If I had the choice between doing something that brought me pleasure or something that created pain, I'd almost always choose the pain, earnestly believing that God always prefers agony over joy. When I didn't choose the more painful path, I'd make up for it with additional suffering later on, even if it that meant just mentally berating myself for the failure of my flesh to have suffered in the first place!

Needless to say, my choices were not always the healthiest mentally, emotionally, or spiritually, and I visited numerous counselors for depression and anxiety. Worst of all, my quest to suffer never made me feel more loved by God, but rather made me feel like I was too worthless to be loved. So I would try a little harder to suffer my way to God's love, becoming trapped in an endless and increasing cycle of pain—all in the pursuit of holiness.

I finally reached a breaking point. My marriage had ended, I had issues within my family, and I had been diagnosed with a chronic, incurable illness. If suffering and adversity were going to make God love me, I should have felt like the most beloved woman on the planet. However, I didn't feel that way. I was angry and sad—almost suicidal. Since I knew that depression, anger, and sorrow weren't fruits of the Holy Spirit, it began to dawn on me that something had to be wrong. So I took a long look at what I was doing in my life. Over the course of several years (I'm a bit of a slow learner), I realized that while I was certainly suffering, it didn't appear that my pain was causing God and the angels to dance in heaven. Worst of all, I knew that I had never actually felt God's love, despite all the penances I had performed.

Suffering and God's Love for Us

About that time, I realized that I simultaneously held two contradictory beliefs. First, I believed that God loves suffering and wants us to experience as much pain as possible because our pain pleases him. Second, I believed that God loves us unconditionally, beyond anything we can imagine. This had all seemed logical to me until I thought about it more deeply and compared my ideas to the love that I have for my own son. It was only then that I began to understand that something was very wrong with my understanding of suffering and God's love. When I love someone, I don't want him or her to needlessly suffer. (I don't even want my cats to suffer, much less the people in my life!) Sometimes suffering is unavoidable, but I certainly would not be pleased if my son were to seek out ways to suffer under the mistaken notion that his pain would make me love him more. What if, as a little boy, he had come to me and said, "Look, Mommy, I've just broken all my toys to make myself very sad because I know that my sadness will make you love me more"? I would have been horrified. If that was true for me, then how much more must it be true for God, since my ability to love is only a shadow of divine love.

That's when I began to question the flaws in my original premise. What if God doesn't really love suffering in and of itself? What if God didn't actually want Jesus to suffer but knew that suffering was the only way that Jesus could accomplish his mission on earth? What if (gasp!) suffering, particularly self-created suffering, isn't the fast track to heaven?

I went back and reread John 16:33 with new eyes: "In the world you will have trouble [suffering], but take courage, I have conquered the world!" (NAB). All of a sudden, it struck me that suffering isn't created by God. God isn't rubbing his proverbial hands with glee every time someone experiences sorrow or pain. In fact, Jesus seemed to be saying, "Yes, you are going to have pain and adversity while you are living on earth, but don't let that get you down, because suffering comes from the world and I've beaten everything that the world can throw at you."

This startling thought led me to the inevitable question: If God doesn't like suffering and adversity, if God isn't the author of it, then why do we all suffer? Of course, humanity has been seeking the answer to that question since ancient times.

In April 2011, after the devastating earthquake and tsunami in Japan, a young Japanese girl asked Pope Benedict XVI a similar question: "Why do I have to be so afraid? Why do children have to be so sad?" The pope replied, "I also have the same questions: Why is it this way? Why do you have to suffer so much while others live in ease?"[1]

In the dark nights of our souls, all of us—even the pope—ask, "Why?"

One answer has always been that we suffer because we sin, personally and collectively. That is often the case. Because of our sin, we create situations in which we must bear the consequences of our actions, be it health issues because of gluttony, destruction of relationships because of infidelity, or loss of the earth's natural resources because of pollution. But as I thought about the idea that we might suffer because we sin or that suffering is somehow the punishment for sin, I came up against a problem—one that the psalmists also struggled with. What about those people who seem to sin with impunity and really don't appear to suffer much because of it? In fact, they are often rewarded with wealth, power, and prestige. (We'll leave the topic of eternal justice and suffering in the next life to another time.) Not to mention that sin doesn't account for the suffering that occurs from natural disasters like the one experienced by the young Japanese girl.

Finally, there were those saints I had heard so much about as a child. Anyone who has read even a few biographies of the saints knows that all experienced some form of adversity. Some endured sickness, physical disabilities, and bodily or emotional pain; others suffered persecution, beatings, and torture from enemies of the Church; still others, rejection by brothers and sisters or rash judgment by superiors. Since the saints were doing their utmost to avoid wrongdoing, the idea that personal suffering is a punishment resulting from sin—while providing part of the answer—wasn't satisfactory. If it were true, the saints should suffer the least of all of us; not, as is often the case, the most.

LESSONS TO BE LEARNED

Since my fundamental misconceptions about suffering began with the stories of the saints, I returned to them to consider what they actually did with their suffering. The first thing I discovered was that by and large, the saints never cried out to God,

"Why me?" but rather, "What lesson would you have me learn, my God?" This was a major "Aha!" moment for me. The saints viewed their suffering as a divine teacher. They turned their pain into lessons for personal growth into holiness. (Sometimes, in their zeal to learn whatever lessons God had planned, they took on additional suffering to speed up the process, which may or may not have been what God had intended.) They understood that whatever comes into our lives arrives in order to help us learn the lessons that we were created to learn in this lifetime. They didn't see adversity as an end but rather as a means to an end. Suffering was the medicine prescribed by the Divine Physician in order to heal the sicknesses of the soul that affect all of us who live within the confines of time and space. St. Thérèse of Lisieux put it succinctly when she said that God is actually pained when we have to suffer but knows that it is necessary for our growth.

Moreover, the saints didn't view their suffering as a way to make God love them but rather as one of the methods that God had allowed to refine, shape, and guide them into wholeness and holiness. Sometimes biographers record that saints used suffering as a way to demonstrate their love of God, but the more I read, the more I understood that the saints embraced suffering, not necessarily to demonstrate love to God (although in some times and cultures that did play a role), but in order to increase their ability to love and be loved so that they could bring more of God's grace to a hurting world.

The difference between those two positions might be subtle but it is critical. If we suffer because we think, as I did for so many years, that it will make God love us, we suffer for nothing.

It's pointless because God will always love us, in our pain and in our pleasure alike. If, however, we accept adversity as a way to grow in our capacity to both give and receive love by learning the lessons that it affords us, then we will experience a greater share of God's love and grace and become more closely united with God's nature.

Looking at it that way, Colossians 1:24 made new sense to me: "I am now rejoicing in my sufferings for your sake, and in my flesh I am completing what is lacking in Christ's afflictions for the sake of his body, that is, the church." The work of renewing the earth, of transforming humanity, isn't something that was done once and for all but is part of the mission and duty of each one of us. We cooperate with the divine in completing that work. When we suffer—and we will all suffer at one point or another in our lives—we are changed. When that change opens us to becoming a greater channel of grace, we can transmit the gift of that transformation to others. We become the new reality we want the world to experience, so in some mysterious way, we really do complete the work of Christ through the acceptance of our adversity and pain.

One more thing: The saints may have experienced pain, even incredible agony, but they rarely "suffered" as I thought of the word. More often than not, they expressed joy, even when they were being tortured! When I was inflicting suffering on myself, I never found any joy in it, so I figured that the saints were either a lot better than I am (which they are, but that's beside the point) or that their hagiographers were putting a pious gloss on their stories (which I still suspect may be true in some cases). As I looked more deeply into their accounts, however, I came to believe that the saints were able to genuinely feel joy and even pleasure simultaneously with adversity because they did not experience suffering as meaningless agony. They understood that God does not relish pointless pain, and, in fact, they comprehended that God is not the creator of our suffering. (How could the source of all that is good create something evil? It is incompatible with the divine nature, no matter what well-meaning people might try to tell us.)

It's true that God does sometimes allow painful events to unfold in our lives. But he also gives us the opportunity to grow from them, perhaps in a way that will help us to fulfill his purposes in our lives. And even if we've created our own suffering because of the choices we've made with the gift of our free will, God can bring good out of evil, and there are still lessons that we can draw from that.

The Choices We Face

So when we experience suffering and adversity, our choices are actually fairly simple: We can choose to stay stuck in the pain (rendering it meaningless), or we can choose to learn from it and move on. Sometimes if we've created the suffering through choices of our own, we move on by asking forgiveness for our mistake and simply letting it go. If the suffering is something that has been allowed by God, such as an illness or accident, "moving on" may mean letting go of our ego-driven need to show God how much we can take. In some instances, it may even mean releasing our lives into death, which is the ultimate "moving on." In any event, "moving on" means not becoming stuck in the suffering itself but, instead, seeing it as part of a greater journey of the soul.

This is what makes saints saintly. They see the pain in their lives as something to be used rather than as something to be endured. Because their pain has purpose, they transform the straw of suffering into the gold of growth in holiness, and as they experience this process, they feel the kind of joy that comes only from knowing the real meaning of life.

Another revelation I had regarding adversity and the saints was that suffering is deeply rooted in our own perceptions. In many cases, suffering is what we make of something. What is painful to one person might be a minor inconvenience to another. When we look at what appears to be incredible suffering in the lives of others, we are always filtering their experiences through our own lenses. And those lenses are colored, not just by our personal standards, but by the time and culture as well.

This is especially important to remember when we look at the lives of the saints. Now, please understand that I'm not attempting to minimize their suffering but rather to place it in context. Take my own patron, Rose of Lima. Although using lye to destroy her beauty was probably a bit extreme even for seventeenth-century Peru, her action was seen by her spiritual advisors as evidence of great piety and something to be respected, if not emulated. Any young girl rubbing pepper and lye on her face today would immediately be put in the hospital for extensive evaluation and therapy. She definitely would not be considered an exceptionally holy woman! However, because Rose's action was seen as holy and pleasing to God by the citizens of Lima, she didn't experience the same kind of "pain" that you or I would have suffered had we done the same thing. It was her perception of the reason for her suffering that made it bearable (and even noble) for her.

Taking her actions or the actions of any saint of long ago out of context creates two problems. First, if we judge their actions by our own feelings, we fail to understand the important meaning behind their adversity. We may become tempted to dismiss their behavior as foolish or even crazy. Second, if we attempt to imitate their behavior, we may subject ourselves to suffering that God does not intend for us who live in the twenty-first century. What's important for us is not so much the precise *actions* of the saints as their *reactions* to suffering, which can serve as our guides and models today.

That is the purpose of this book: to help you find a way to transform your suffering by looking not at *how* the saints suffered but *what* they did with their adversities to grow both in wholeness as human beings and in holiness as expressions of God's creative love. By using their lives as inspiration, I hope that you, too, will find the courage, in the words of Pope Benedict to the young Japanese girl, to "know that Jesus suffered as you do, an innocent, and that the true God who is revealed in Jesus is by your side."[2]

FOR CONSIDERATION

1. What have I been taught about suffering? Have I ever believed that God likes people to suffer? Are any of the ideas that I have embraced inaccurate or unhelpful? Am I willing to let go of those ideas, even if I've clung to them for a long time?

2. Do I think that I must suffer in order to be loved by God? Can I reframe my suffering by thinking about it in a different way?

3. In the midst of my pain, when have I asked God, "Why?" When have I asked, "What am I to learn?" What was the result?

4. When have I created any unnecessary suffering or adversity in my life? Did I realize that I was doing so?

5. If any of my suffering is the result of sin, have I asked for forgiveness?

6. Have I ever made my family and friends suffer because of my own suffering? If so, have I asked for their forgiveness?

7. How might I be "stuck" in my suffering? Could a trusted friend, family member, or my pastor help me if I am unable to move beyond my pain?

8. How can I use my suffering to complete the work of renewing the world that was begun in Christ?

Prayer

in Time of Suffering (Psalm 23)

The LORD is my shepherd, I shall not want.
  He makes me lie down in green pastures;
he leads me beside still waters;
  he restores my soul.
He leads me in right paths
  for his name's sake.

Even though I walk through the darkest valley,
  I fear no evil;
for you are with me;
  your rod and your staff—
  they comfort me.

You prepare a table before me
  in the presence of my enemies;
you anoint my head with oil;
  my cup overflows.
Surely goodness and mercy shall follow me
  all the days of my life,
and I shall dwell in the house of the LORD
  my whole life long.

Chapter 2

Physical Pain
St. Pio of Pietrelcina (Padre Pio)

As we look at the ways saints dealt with adversity, physical pain is a good place to start since almost everyone has experienced physical pain at some time in their lives. In fact, many other types of suffering, such as torture, hunger, disability, and even mental anguish, are expressed physically. Pain is one of the common denominators of humanity.

You'd be hard-pressed to find a saint who didn't suffer physically in some form or another. Sometimes the pain was the result of illness or injury; at other times it was the result of self-mortification, and especially in the past, it was often the result of torture.

Padre Pio (May 25, 1887–September 23, 1968) is a good role model for physical suffering for us today because he is a contemporary saint and one of the most popular of modern times. A Capuchin priest, Padre Pio is famous for bearing the stigmata, the marks of Christ's passion, for more than fifty years. The pain he experienced from the open wounds was intense and unending. This is how he described it in a letter to his spiritual advisor in 1918:

> Imagine the agony I experienced and continue to experience almost every day. The heart wound bleeds continually, especially from Thursday evening until Saturday. Dear

Father, I am dying of pain because of the wounds and the resulting embarrassment I feel deep in my soul. I am afraid I shall bleed to death if the Lord does not hear my heartfelt supplication to relieve me of this condition. Will Jesus, who is so good, grant me this grace? Will he at least free me from the embarrassment caused by these outward signs? I will raise my voice and will not stop imploring him until in his mercy he takes away, not the wound or the pain, which is impossible since I wish to be inebriated with pain, but these outward signs which cause me such embarrassment and unbearable humiliation.[1]

While the wounds of the stigmata were the most obvious of Padre Pio's torments, his other physical sufferings are not as well-known. According to his spiritual director, he was bedridden from a grave gastroenteritis at age six. He had typhoid fever at age ten. When he was seventeen, he experienced exhaustion, fainting spells, migraines, and severe nausea. He also had "asthmatic bronchitis," kidney stones, ulcers, inflammation of the ear, nose, and throat, pulmonary tuberculosis, an inguinal hernia, a large cyst on his neck, cancer on his ear, pleurisy, and arthritis.

In addition to this long list, he experienced the spiritual phenomenon called "transverberation," which was described by St. John of the Cross in this way: "It will happen that while the soul is inflamed with the love of God, . . . it will feel that a seraph is assailing it by means of an arrow or dart that is all afire with love."[2] Padre Pio says this about the experience:

While I was hearing the boys' confessions on the evening of the 5th [August], I was suddenly terrorized by the sight of a celestial person who presented himself to my mind's eye. He had in his hand a sort of weapon like a very long sharp-pointed steel blade which seemed to emit fire. At the very instant that I saw all this, I saw that person hurl the weapon into my soul with all his might. I cried out with difficulty and felt I was dying. I asked the boy to leave because I felt ill and no longer had the strength to continue. This agony lasted uninterruptedly until the morning of the 7th. I cannot tell you how much I suffered during this period of anguish. Even my entrails were torn and ruptured by the weapon, and nothing was spared. From that day on I have been mortally wounded. I feel in the depths of my soul a wound that is always open and which causes me continual agony.[3]

What makes Padre Pio a useful guide for our purposes is that unlike saints who were born when medical treatment was rudimentary, he was both willing and able to utilize modern medicine to help alleviate that suffering caused by illness. For example, he successfully underwent both surgery and radiation treatment for the cancer on his ear and was treated for tuberculosis. However, as anyone who suffers from illness or disease knows, modern medicine is hardly a panacea since it cannot always remove the pain and sometimes actually creates more pain. Moreover, although Padre Pio did suffer from some extraordinary types of pain that most of us will never experience, such as the stigmata and transverberation, he also had his share of "ordinary" pain, such as arthritis and infections.

So what can we learn and apply to our own lives from the example of Padre Pio?

First, what enabled Padre Pio to wish to be "inebriated with pain" was not masochism but a profound understanding that divine intent lay beneath his suffering. He knew that one of his life purposes was to show the modern world how to suffer without becoming insufferable. While we may not be called to such intense redemptive suffering, we can use Padre Pio's example to accept our pain, whatever it might be, with grace. "St. Pio . . . was a man who suffered in many ways," says Brother Loarne of the National Shrine of St. Pio in Pantasaph, North Wales, "but because he discovered that all of life has a purpose, he found a deep joy and lasting peace that he wanted to share with others."[4]

When you are able to see your suffering in the light of life's greater purpose, your suffering becomes redemptive rather than destructive. As long as you believe your suffering is without merit, it will do nothing for your spiritual growth. It is only when you realize that physical suffering can become a means to holiness that it can be transformed from mere pain into peaceful acceptance. This is the first lesson we can learn from the example of Padre Pio.

KEEPING IT QUIET

Second, we've all known people who feel obliged to tell you all their symptoms, solicit constant sympathy, and complain unceasingly. And we all know just how frustrating and annoying those people can be. If you are experiencing physical pain, make a decision to keep quiet about it. Be like Padre Pio, who throughout his life kept the stigmata hidden under gloves and refused to discuss it despite the constant pain. Of course, this doesn't mean that you should ignore symptoms or leave your illnesses untreated—Padre Pio didn't do that, and neither should you. It does mean that when asked how you are, you don't begin with a long litany of misery but simply smile or say something like "Fine, thank you" or "I'm doing the best I can."

That's not just good spiritual advice; it's also good medical advice. Scientific studies have shown that constantly talking about your pain and focusing on it will cause your perception of it to increase. In other words, the more you think about it, the more it hurts. The opposite is also true. We've all had the experience of becoming so involved in something that we forget ourselves. The point is that when we are engrossed in meaningful activities, we are much better able to withstand discomfort. Getting our minds off ourselves is healthy spiritually, emotionally, and physically!

Keeping his pain to himself was a hallmark of Padre Pio's life. Even as his health deteriorated, he continued to say Mass and hear confessions without ever turning attention to himself. A good example of this came the day before his death. He was supposed to say a high Mass but felt too weak, so he asked his superior if he could say a low Mass instead. When the superior told him to continue with the high Mass, Padre Pio didn't whine and complain but simply did as he was told. (I suspect the superior felt rather bad about the whole thing when he realized that Padre Pio was actually dying!) Moving your focus and intent onto what you can do for others instead of what you are experiencing is a major step in the acceptance of physical suffering and a key component in its being transformed into a blessing rather than a curse.

ACCEPTING WHAT WE CAN'T CHANGE

Finally, probably without ever actually knowing the words, Padre Pio clearly applied the Serenity Prayer to his physical afflictions. (Actually, the Serenity Prayer is a good guide for all those who are suffering since it puts pain into a heavenly rather than earthly perspective.)

> God, grant me the serenity to accept the things
>   I cannot change,
> Courage to change the things I can,
> And wisdom to know the difference.

Padre Pio apparently did pray early on to be released from the stigmata, but when he realized that it was totally out of his control and had come into his life because God had ordained it, he embraced the pain and did not let it become an undue hindrance to his mission in life. On the other hand, he knew that he could correct his inguinal hernia through medical intervention, and so he acted in accord with his doctor's advice. For him, as for all of us, having the wisdom to know which aspects of our physical suffering are out of our control and which can be legitimately addressed is essential. Remember, God does not love physical pain for the sake of pain. God did not give Padre Pio the stigmata or transverberation or arthritis or cancer out of sadism or cruelty, and he doesn't do that to us either. Here is how another great contemporary saint, Thérèse of Lisieux, explained it:

> Never does our suffering make Him happy, but it is necessary for us, and so He sends it to us, while, as it were, turning away His face. . . . I assure you that it costs Him dearly to fill us with bitterness. The good God, who so loves us, has pain enough in being obliged to leave us on earth to fulfill our time of trial, without our constantly telling Him of our discomfort; we must appear not to notice it. . . . Far from complaining to Our Lord of the cross which He sends us, I cannot fathom the infinite love which has led Him to treat us this way. . . . What a favor from Jesus, and how He must love us to send us so great a sorrow! Eternity will not be long enough to bless Him for it.[5]

The physical pain that he experienced was part of Padre Pio's greater mission, and our pain is often part of our mission as well. In other words, for reasons we don't fully understand, Padre Pio needed to have his pain in order to become the saint he is today, and we may need our pain in order to become a saint tomorrow. Because Padre Pio understood the greater good behind the pain, he could accept his physical suffering and still live a life of joy and blessing. We must do the same. We must not blame God for inflicting physical suffering on us but instead realize the truths expressed in these words of the great poet Kahil Gibran: "Your pain . . . is the bitter potion by which the physician within you heals your sick self. Therefore trust the physician, and drink his remedy in silence and tranquility: For his hand, though heavy and hard, is guided by the tender hand of the Unseen."[6]

FOR CONSIDERATION

1. What lesson might God intend for me to learn through my physical suffering? How can my pain help me to grow in holiness?

2. Can I see a link between my pain and my life's purpose? Have I asked God to show me if there is such a link?

3. How often do I let pain dictate my life? Can I find a way to transcend my physical discomfort in order to focus more on matters of the soul? What aspect of my pain might I be making worse by focusing on it?

4. How can I best take care of my responsibilities to myself and my family in spite of my pain? What else might I do, medically speaking, to get more relief? Is something stopping me from seeking out help?

5. If I have ever been guilty of "enjoying" ill health in order to gain sympathy, what was my motivation? How could drawing closer to God in prayer achieve the same purpose?

6. If I have created any of my physical suffering through my own actions, have I confessed my fault and asked for forgiveness?

7. Have I asked God for healing? If not, why not?

8. If I have asked for healing and it hasn't come, do I still maintain hope that God will heal me eventually? If I am still in pain, have I asked for the grace to endure my suffering as Padre Pio did?

9. How do I deal with the pain of others? Am I compassionate? Am I patient?

Prayer

OF ST. PIO OF PIETRELCINA AFTER HOLY COMMUNION

Stay with me, Lord, for it is necessary to have You present
    so that I do not forget You.
    You know how easily I abandon You.
Stay with me, Lord, because I am weak and I need Your
    strength, that I may not fall so often.
Stay with me, Lord, for You are my life,
    and without You, I am without fervor.
Stay with me, Lord, for You are my light,
    and without You, I am in darkness.
Stay with me, Lord, to show me Your will.
Stay with me, Lord, so that I hear Your voice
    and follow You.
Stay with me, Lord, for I desire to love You very much,
    and always be in Your company.

Stay with me, Lord, if You wish me to be faithful to You.
Stay with me, Lord, for as poor as my soul is, I want it to
    be a place of consolation for You, a nest of love.

Stay with me, Jesus, for it is getting late and the day is
    coming to a close,
    and life passes; death, judgment, eternity approaches.
It is necessary to renew my strength,
    so that I will not stop along the way and for that, I
    need You.
It is getting late and death approaches, I fear the darkness,
    the temptations, the dryness, the cross, the sorrows.
O how I need You, my Jesus, in this night of exile!
Stay with me tonight, Jesus, in life with all its dangers.
    I need You.

Let me recognize You as Your disciples did at the
    breaking of the bread,
so that the Eucharistic Communion be the Light which
    disperses the darkness,
    the force which sustains me,
    the unique joy of my heart.
Stay with me, Lord, because at the hour of my death,
    I want to remain united to You,
    if not by communion, at least by grace and love.
Stay with me, Jesus, I do not ask for divine consolation,
    because I do not merit it,
    but the gift of Your Presence, oh yes, I ask this of You!

Stay with me, Lord, for it is You alone I look for,
    Your Love, Your Grace, Your Will, Your Heart,
    Your Spirit,
    because I love You and ask no other reward but to love
    You more and more.
With a firm love, I will love You with all my heart while
    on earth,
And continue to love You perfectly during all eternity.
Amen.[7]

CHAPTER 3

Mental Suffering

BLESSED TERESA OF KOLCATA

One of the iconic images of the twentieth century is a tiny woman in a white and blue sari walking the slums of India, caring for the sick and dying. Blessed Teresa of Kolcata (August 26, 1910–September 5, 1997), or Mother Teresa of Calcutta as she is more commonly known, was proclaimed a living saint long before her death from heart failure. As the foundress of the Missionaries of Charity, her work took her around the globe. Wherever she went, she brought attention to the plight of the least, the lonely, the impoverished, and the unloved. Many of her sayings, such as "Loneliness is the most terrible poverty" and "Love is a fruit in season at all times," have become bywords for those who work for social justice and compassionate treatment of the poorest of the poor.

One of the hallmarks of Mother Teresa's life was her almost constant smile. Virtually everyone who met her noticed the joy and peace that emanated from her. She seemed to have perfect faith and trust in God and his will throughout her entire life. Many openly talked about how they wished they could have the kind of faith that characterized her life.

However, after her death, her postulator, Fr. Brian Kolodiejchuk, revealed that for nearly fifty years, she did not feel the presence of God in her life. For most of that time, she suffered from what St. John of the Cross called the "dark night of the soul," a sense of profound desolation, loneliness, and abandonment shared by other saints, including St. Thérèse of Lisieux. This is how Mother Teresa described her suffering:

Where is my faith?—Even deep down, . . . there is nothing but emptiness & darkness. . . . I have no faith. . . . If there be God, please forgive me. . . . When I try to raise my thoughts to Heaven—there is such convicting emptiness that those very thoughts return like sharp knives and hurt my very soul.—Love—the word—it brings nothing.— I am told God loves me—and yet the reality of darkness & coldness & emptiness is so great that nothing touches my soul.[1]

What do I labour for? If there be no God—there can be no soul.—If there be no soul then, Jesus—You also are not true.[2]

About ten years into her pain, she experienced a short reprieve during which she was relieved of "that long darkness, . . . that strange suffering." However, the darkness and doubt returned and, so far as anyone knows, remained with her until the day she died.

Mother Teresa's mental pain and suffering come as a surprise to many people who assume that saints never have to endure the mental and emotional anguish that so many of us "ordinary" people have to face. From her experience, we can draw several lessons that can help us as we progress on our own journey to understand and deal with suffering and adversity.

One of the first is that love of God and devotion to faith don't automatically eliminate the pain of mental suffering. Mental suffering isn't the same as mental illness, which is another kind of suffering altogether. Mental suffering is the pain that comes with doubt, fear, and anxiety. Often it appears disguised under the cloak of "worry." While it might be a bit presumptuous to suggest that a holy woman like Mother Teresa worried, the writings that she had not wanted to be revealed lest "people will think more of me—less of Jesus" hint that she did indeed worry. She worried that she had not heard God correctly when he told her to serve the poorest of the poor; she worried that her life might have been spent in vain; she even worried that there might not be a God.

Worry is one of those forms of suffering that is so common that we almost assume it is a universal condition of being human. However, one of the few direct commands given by Jesus in the New Testament forbids it: "So do not worry about tomorrow, for tomorrow will bring worries of its own. Today's trouble is enough for today" (Matthew 6:34).

Don't Wrestle with Worry

What is key here seems to be the difference between the emotion of worry, which arrives on the threshold of our minds unbidden and unwanted, and deliberate wallowing in our fearful fretting. I believe that Jesus was admonishing us against the latter, not the former. If that's the case, then Mother Teresa gives us an insightful example of how we should treat suffering that is the result of the emotion of worry: Release it and get on with the next right thing in our lives. We are not to wrestle with it over and over, like a dog with a stuffed toy. Instead, we are to recognize it, accept it, and go on with our duties.

Now, I realize that when you are "worried sick" about something, such advice is easier said than done. But in the end, worry accomplishes nothing. It merely gives the illusion of action when in reality, it is a way of remaining stuck in your misery. It may feel as if you are busy doing something when you worry, but all you are actually doing is wasting your time, energy, and emotional resources. Mother Teresa seemed to intuitively understand this because even when she was experiencing her most profound darkness, she continued to pray, serve the poor, beam that radiant smile, and go about her daily routine.

That is exactly what we need to do when we are in the grips of mental suffering—keep on with our lives. You may be worried about your financial situation, but if the dishes need to be done, do the dishes instead of stewing and fretting about what might happen tomorrow. You may be facing a troubling medical diagnosis, but if dinner needs to be made while you wait for the phone call, make dinner. You may be pacing the floor, wondering if a loved one has been in an accident, but if the cat needs to be fed, feed the cat. Do the right thing, then the next right thing, and then the next one. In short, what Mother Teresa's example teaches us is that we should take concrete action when we are in the grip of suffering generated by worry. Sometimes as we continue to do the next right thing, our troublesome situation is resolved on its own. Even if whatever is worrying us can't be completely resolved, doing what is right in the present moment makes it much easier to bear the pain that accompanies the emotion of worry because it takes the emphasis off ourselves and our situations and places it on our God-given duties and responsibilities. When we aren't thinking about ourselves, it's much more difficult to worry, and it's almost impossible to become overwhelmed by worry when we leave the situation in God's hands.

One more lesson we can learn about mental suffering from Mother Teresa is to keep it private. It's tempting to want to talk about your pain in the hope that by telling everyone, you can somehow dissipate it. The opposite is actually the case. The more you talk about your worries and suffering, the greater they will seem. Now, certainly it can be beneficial to talk with a counselor or spiritual director—Mother Teresa did that herself—but sharing your worries with the whole world isn't wise. It's far better to select your confidante with care, choosing someone who can advise you and not merely commiserate with you. In the absence of such wise counsel, journaling about your concerns, as Mother Teresa did, is often one of the better ways of dealing with this particular type of suffering because it allows you to examine the issue more objectively (although if you are planning on becoming a saint, you can't be sure that your private journals will always remain private!).

COMBATING FEAR

Another aspect of Mother Teresa's mental suffering that is an example for us is her resolve and courage in combating fear. One of the most insidious aspects of mental suffering is that it often paralyzes us with fear. Someone once said that fear is nothing more than "false evidence appearing real." It would have been easy for Mother Teresa to succumb to the idea that since she no longer felt the presence of God, God was displeased with her or even nonexistent. However, that "fear" would have been nothing more than "false evidence appearing real." While she undoubtedly experienced a great deal of anguish from her thoughts, she did not let those fearful thoughts rule her life. In fact, when asked by *Time* magazine what her greatest fear was, she answered, "I have Jesus, I have no fear."[3] In light of what we now know about her mental suffering, such a statement is remarkable! However, we may be able to get a glimpse of the worry that she was combating when a few moments later she was asked about her plans for the future, and she replied in words that suspiciously echo Matthew 6:34: "I just take one day. Yesterday is gone. Tomorrow has not come. We have only today to love Jesus."

As we look at the life of Mother Teresa, something else about her attitude toward suffering needs to examined, that is, her so-called theology of suffering. Mother Teresa was famous for saying that "pain, sorrow, suffering are but the kiss of Jesus—a sign that you have come so close to Him that he can kiss you." In looking at Mother Teresa's life and the mental suffering she endured, it isn't difficult to see why she developed a particular theology that put an emphasis on accepting suffering, especially physical suffering, with open arms.

She knew that she was offering her entire life to God as a gift, and she also knew that she was in great mental anguish for most of it. She also must have been aware that her "dark night" was like that of John of the Cross, who as a way of mortifying the passions, recommended the following:

Endeavor to be included always:
not to the easiest, but to the most difficult;
not to the most delightful, but to the most distasteful;
not to the most gratifying, but to the less pleasant;
not to what means rest for you, but to hard work;
not to the consoling, but to the unconsoling;
not the most, but to the least;
not the highest and most precious, but to the lowest and
    most despised;
not to wanting something, but to wanting nothing."[4]

She clearly modeled her life and that of her sisters on that credo. But one of the problems in the spiritual life is that we are often tempted to assume that a personal experience is universal. Mother Teresa was able to transform her pain into a love offering to God, so it's not out of the question for us to think that everyone would be as capable of transforming suffering as she was.

Yet God deals with each of us as individuals, including the suffering that he allows in our lives. Offering up pain is one of the major lessons we can learn from the saints, especially Mother Teresa. But we also shouldn't assume that everyone else can or should experience suffering in the same way we do.

What that means on a practical level in our own families is that while we may undertake certain disciplines (such as rising early for prayer or fasting), it's not our right to insist that our spouses or children share those disciplines. All suffering, both that allowed by God and that created by our own choices, is always unique to the individual. Because of that, we shouldn't think that others should share in our unique suffering or view it in the same way. Rest assured, they will find ample opportunity on their own!

Mother Teresa's mental sufferings came as a surprise, even to those who worked with her, because she did not allow the pain of her doubt and "dark night" to take over her life or highjack her mission in life. Nor must we, when we experience worry, anxiety, or fear, allow those negative influences to prevent us from doing what we have been created to do. If we learn no other lesson from Mother Teresa than this, it would be enough.

FOR CONSIDERATION

1. When I realize I am worrying about something, what do I do? Do I do the "next right thing," or do I remain stuck in my pattern of fretting? Do I lift up my concern to the Lord and let it go, or do I let it fester and cause anxiety? What would help me remember to bring my worries to the Lord?

2. In what ways is my fear actually "false evidence appearing real"? What role does Satan, the father of lies, play in fanning the flames of my fear? How could prayer help?

3. When I am suffering mentally, do I keep it private, or do I talk about it to everyone I encounter? What are the benefits of discussing my fear, worry, or anxiety with only my spouse, spiritual director, or counselor? In what ways could that lessen my suffering?

4. How resolved am I to combat worry and fear? How can Scripture help in that regard? How can the sacraments help?

5. What is one lesson I have learned after suffering from excessive fear or worry? What was God trying to teach me? What lessons might he have for me now?

6. If I am suffering mentally, have I investigated the possibility of an illness, such as depression, as a root cause for my suffering? How might appropriate medical help alleviate my pain?

7. Since Jesus has told us not to worry, is it possible that my worrying is causing me to sin? Have I talked to my priest in confession about it and asked for divine aid in removing worry from my life? How can I grow more in trusting the Lord?

Prayer
AGAINST FEAR AND WORRY

O Christ Jesus,
when all is darkness
and we feel our weakness and helplessness,
give us the sense of your presence,
your love, and your strength.
Help us to have perfect trust
in your protecting love
and strengthening power,
so that nothing may frighten or worry us,
for, living close to you,
we shall see your hand,
your purpose, your will through all things.
　　　—St. Ignatius Loyola

—CHAPTER 4—

Physical Disabilities

ST. ALPHONSUS LIGUORI

Many saints have suffered from physical disabilities. Blessed Margaret of Castello suffered from dwarfism as well as a hunched back and other deformities. St. Gerald of Aurillac was blind. St. Servulus was afflicted with such severe palsy that he couldn't stand or even sit without assistance.

While all of these saints undoubtedly can teach us lessons about living with the suffering that results from physical disabilities, it is St. Alphonsus Liguori (September 27, 1696–August 1, 1787) who we are going to look at in this chapter. The reason is simple: He handled the suffering involved with his disabilities so well that most people are unaware that he had severe physical limitations.

The founder of the Redemptorists Order, St. Alphonsus was not healthy, to say the least; he received the Last Rites eight times during his long life. (He lived to be ninety-one.) While he suffered from various afflictions, his greatest disability was the result of rheumatic fever, which left him at least partially paralyzed. The most notable evidence of this illness was a severely bent head that can be seen in some of his later portraits. It was so crooked that his chin created a deep sore on his chest and he was forced to drink through a straw. The only way he could say Mass was to support himself on a chair and allow an acolyte to help him raise the chalice to his lips. He also suffered from arthritis as well as being extremely myopic at a time when glasses and corrective lenses were hardly what they are today. Finally, in his later years, he went almost completely deaf.

Despite these physical problems, St. Alphonsus was a prolific author, compassionate pastor, and courageous founder of a religious order. His erudition, practical faith, and devotion to Mary led to his being named one of the doctors of the Church, and his pithy advice still brings comfort and consolation to many. Among his many oft-quoted statements is his admonition not to approach God in terror but to draw near with loving confidence:

> It is a great mistake . . . to be afraid of Him and to act in His presence like a timid and craven slave trembling with fright before his master. . . . Just as a mother finds pleasure in taking her little child on her lap, there to feed and caress him, in like manner our loving God shows His fondness for His beloved souls who have given themselves entirely to Him and have placed all their hope in His goodness.[1]

While we cannot know the reasons why God allowed St. Alphonsus to experience so many physical limitations, his actions and reactions to his suffering can serve to inspire and guide us as we cope with our own physical limitations.

TALKING TO GOD

One of the first lessons we can learn from St. Alphonsus is to take our pain to God. Most people get tired of hearing us talk about our pain, but God is the compassionate friend who always listens. Because formal prayer often isn't adequate to express our feelings, St. Alphonsus urges us simply to talk to God. As he wrote, "Speak to Him often of your business, your plans, your troubles, your fears—of everything that concerns you." Instead of burdening our family and friends with our complaints, we can always take those complaints to God. "Ask those who love Him with a sincere love," he wrote, "and they will tell you that they find no greater or prompter relief amid the troubles of their life than in loving conversation with their Divine Friend."

One warning: When you talk to God about your suffering, don't expect a satisfactory answer to the questions "Why?" or "Why me?" (even though all of us ask this at some time in our lives). The lack of an answer is not because God is incapable of giving us a response but because our capacity for comprehension is limited. It's a bit like a toddler asking his mother why the sky is blue. The toddler isn't going to understand the scientific answer about the scattering of certain wavelengths that correspond to the color blue. Many times God's answer to our "Why do I have to suffer?" would be just as incomprehensible to us as a scientific explanation for a blue sky would be to a small child.

I'll admit that when I was diagnosed with a chronic, incurable, but not fatal illness that stripped me of my ability to do many of the physical activities I had enjoyed, I did not become the poster child for gracious acceptance or courage. I felt sorry for myself, I complained, and I asked "Why?" many times. However, I eventually learned that asking "Why?" got me nowhere. I got scientific answers relating to "substance P," neurotransmitters, and other polysyllabic medical terms, but the real why—"Why did this happen to me?"—was unanswerable. The most any doctor could tell me was a carefully guarded variation of the old parental standby: "Just because."

That's when I learned that instead of asking why, it's far more useful to ask what or how: "What am I to learn from this?" "What am I to do with this?" "How can I use this for my spiritual growth?" Asking what or how will always generate an answer because there is always something we can do once we accept our pain, even if we don't always comprehend the reason behind it. In the words of Lesley Hazelton, the British-American blogger who calls herself "The Accidental Theologist," "Suffering, once accepted, loses its edge, for the terror of it lessens, and what remains is generally far more manageable than we had imagined."

For me, one of the answers to my "What should I do with this?" question was to learn to have more patience with myself, with others, and with life in general. For St. Alphonsus, one of his answers was to give thanks:

Who is there that ever receives a gift and tries to make bargains about it? Let us, then, return thanks for what He has bestowed on us. Who can tell whether, if we had had a larger share of ability or stronger health, we should not have possessed them to our destruction.[2]

Calling suffering in any form a "gift" isn't something most of us do naturally. But many saints, not just Alphonsus, had this reaction. To understand why they would be thankful for their suffering, it may be helpful to understand what "returning thanks" really means. It doesn't mean putting on an ear-to-ear grin and tossing rose petals in the air with joy. Even Jesus didn't do that. He wept, he sweated blood, and he asked if his cup of suffering could be removed. Being thankful in the midst of suffering means that we receive with calm acceptance what has come into our lives, recognizing that God has allowed it for our spiritual growth. It means being grateful, if we can, that it isn't worse. At the very least, it means that we don't waste our time or energy by railing against something that can't be changed, but instead, we determine to fulfill our God-given mission in life to the best of our ability in spite of our physical disabilities.

Fulfilling Our Life's Mission

In that, St. Alphonsus provides a sterling example. He was a brilliant scholar, entering law school at the age of sixteen. As the years went by, he became increasingly unhappy as a lawyer, telling a colleague, "My friend, our profession is too full of difficulties and dangers; we lead an unhappy life and run risk of dying an unhappy death. For myself, I will quit this career, which does not suit me; for I wish to secure the salvation of my soul."[3] After losing his first case at the age of twenty-seven, he left the courts and began a period of intense introspection, which resulted in his ordination. From that point on, he turned his formidable intellect toward the faith. Instead of legal briefs, he wrote devotional and apologetic works—111 of them in all. He worked among the poor in the slums of Naples and other cities, eventually establishing the Congregation of the Most Holy Redeemer, whose members were devoted to preaching and teaching the poor. All the while he was combating the challenges of his physical disabilities, receiving the Last Rites numerous times, and experiencing what one biographer called "a living martyrdom."

If that weren't enough, in 1762 Alphonsus was consecrated Bishop of Sant'Agata dei Goti, a post he did not want. He tried to get out of it, pointing out both his advancing age and his infirmities, to no avail. (Even saints take advantage of legitimate opportunities to stop doing things they dislike!) In the following years, he asked both Popes Clement XIII (1758–69) and Clement XIV (1769–74) to relieve him of his duties, but it wasn't until 1775, when he was nearly eighty, that the newly elected Pius VI allowed him to retire.

Throughout his long life, St. Alphonsus did his duty, whatever it was, despite his physical challenges. However, because of his limitations, he was forced to find creative ways to fulfill his obligations, like having an acolyte assist him with the chalice during Mass. He even used his handicaps to his advantage at times. His biographers report that he loved music, and one of the best places to hear live music at the time was at the theater. However, the theater had a very bad reputation, so St. Alphonsus would go and sit in the back and remove his glasses, secure in the knowledge that his myopia would prevent him from seeing anything scandalous.

Like St. Alphonsus, we are called to both accept our limitations and at the same time do what we can to relieve them. Most important, as the saint himself tells us, we must do our best to fulfill our life's mission, no matter what our physical state:

It is especially necessary that we be resigned in corporal infirmities. We should willingly embrace them in the manner and for the length of time that God wills. We ought to make use of the ordinary remedies in time of sickness—such is God's will; but if they are not effective, let us unite ourselves to God's will and this will be better for us than would be our restoration to health. . . . When our sufferings are excessive, it is not wrong to let our friends know what we are enduring, and also to ask God to free us from our sufferings. Let it be understood, however, that the sufferings here referred to are actually excessive. It often happens that some, on the occasion of a slight illness, or even a slight indisposition, want the whole world to stand still and sympathize with them in their illnesses.

But where it is a case of real suffering, we have the example of our Lord, who, at the approach of his bitter passion, made known his state of soul to his disciples, saying, "My soul is sorrowful even unto death," and besought his eternal Father to deliver him from it: "Father, if it be possible, let this chalice pass from me." But our Lord likewise taught us what we should do when we have made such a petition, when he added: "Nevertheless, not as I will, but as thou wilt."

. . . Many times it will happen that proper medical attention or effective remedies will be lacking, or even that the doctor will not rightly diagnose our case. In such instances we must unite ourselves to the divine will which thus disposes of our physical health.[4]

Finally, the response of St. Alphonsus to the suffering he endured because of his disabilities teaches us, as we discussed in the opening chapter, that the suffering that comes not through any fault of our own but because God wills and allows it can have a profound effect on the world. This appears to have been the case with St. Alphonsus. There was nothing he had done that caused rheumatic fever to distort his body. There was nothing he had done to cause his joints to deform from arthritis or to be extremely nearsighted. Those sufferings were not the result of sin or bad personal choices but pains allowed by God. As a result, even today, more than two hundred years after his death, St. Alphonsus is regarded as one of the world's great spiritual teachers. Through his example we learn that God-ordained pain, when accepted as part of the divine plan that we cannot fully understand, has the power to transform not just our own lives but the lives of many others as well—to send waves of transformation rippling throughout the world.

We have only to look at the stories of people such as Helen Keller, who was both blind and deaf, Franklin D. Roosevelt, who was wheelchair bound after contracting polio, or Pope John Paul II, who had Parkinson's disease, to realize how much we gain by witnessing the triumph of the human spirit over physical limitations. Their stories of courage give us hope that we, too, might find similar courage to face our own limitations.

However, saints like St. Alphonsus (and Blessed John Paul II) do more than demonstrate the power of the human spirit. They teach us that our suffering, when understood as part of the divine plan intended for our spiritual growth, has the power to make us holy. As St. Alphonsus noted in *Conformity to God's Will*, "A single act of conformity with the divine will suffices to make a saint." Since the entire world is constantly moving toward either holiness or hopelessness, each time we take an individual step toward the light, we contribute to the global banishment of the dark—just as St. Alphonsus did then, and continues to help us do today.

FOR CONSIDERATION

1. What mission has God given me to accomplish in my life? How has my disability or any physical limitation that I have hindered or helped me?

2. What creative ways have I found to get around my limitations? How have I enlisted the help of my brothers and sisters in Christ?

3. Do I ever give thanks for my limitations? Why or why not? How can I see my limitation as a gift rather than as a liability?

4. How often do I whine about my pain to family and friends? How can I speak about my limitations to others without complaining?

5. How does my limitation affect my prayer life? Do I talk about it with God? Do I accept it if there is no hope of improvement or a cure? What does God say to me when I am feeling sorry for myself?

6. How can I use my disability as a way to make manifest the power of God to transform suffering into hope?

7. As I look at my life, how has my suffering, my disability, or my limitation contributed to my growth as a person?

Prayer

NOVENA PRAYER TO ST. ALPHONSUS LIGUORI

Glorious St. Alphonsus, Bishop and Doctor of the Church, devoted servant of our Lord and loving child of Mary, I invoke you as a Saint in heaven. I give myself to your protection that you may always be my father, my protector, and my guide in the way of holiness and salvation. Aid me in observing the duties of my state of life. Obtain for me great purity of heart and a fervent love of the interior life after your own example.

Great lover of the Blessed Sacrament and the Passion of Jesus Christ, teach me to love Holy Mass and Holy Communion as the source of grace and holiness. Give me a tender devotion to the Passion of my Redeemer. Promoter of the truth of Christ in your preaching and writing, give me a greater knowledge and appreciation of the Divine truths.

Gentle father of the poor and sinners, help me to imitate your charity toward others in word and deed. Consoler of the suffering, help me to bear my daily cross patiently in imitation of your own patience in your long and painful illness and to resign myself to the will of God.

Good Shepherd of the flock of Christ, obtain for me the grace of being a true child of Holy Mother Church. St. Alphonsus, I humbly implore your powerful intercession for obtaining from the Heart of Jesus all the graces necessary for my spiritual and temporal welfare. I recommend to you in particular this favor: (Mention your request).

I have great confidence in your prayers. I earnestly trust that if it is God's holy will, my petition will be granted through your intercession for me at the throne of God.

St. Alphonsus, pray for me and for those I love. I beg of you, by your love for Jesus and Mary, do not abandon us in our needs. May we experience the peace and joy of your holy death. Amen.[5]

CHAPTER 5

Addictions

VENERABLE MATTHEW TALBOT

Some suffering, like the disabilities of St. Alphonsus Liguori, is simply allowed by God. Other types of adversity result more from our own choices than from forces outside our control. The suffering that comes with addiction is one of the latter. While it can be argued that the propensity for certain types of addiction may have a genetic or generational basis and thus are at least partially permitted by God, addictions still largely depend on our own free will choices.

Before we look at the life of Venerable Matthew Talbot (May 2, 1856–June 7, 1925), the unofficial patron saint of addicts, we need to take a few minutes to talk about addiction in general.

We tend to think of addicts as those in the grasp of drugs or alcohol. But in our most honest moments, even those of us who have not had a drug or alcohol addiction realize that at some time we have experienced some sort of addictive behavior. It's just that some addictions are more culturally and socially acceptable than others. For instance, being "addicted" to exercise is generally seen as a positive. It's only when our addictions fall outside society's approval or cause real harm to us—excessive drinking, gambling, drugs, sexual promiscuity—that we are thought to have a problem.

However, all addictions, even "good" ones, create suffering. A woman who must get in an hour of exercise every day experiences the pain of guilt when forced to skip it. A man who is a workaholic may try to justify his long hours by saying he is providing for his family, but he will undoubtedly encounter the pain of regret when his kids grow up without him. Even the most benign addiction will probably cause us or those around us some pain at some point. (Just try being around someone who has missed his or her morning cup of coffee, and this will become immediately clear!) Those addictions that are physically, mentally, or emotionally harmful are absolutely guaranteed to bring suffering into our lives and the lives of our loved ones.

If we are to live the abundant life that Jesus said he came to give us (John 10:10), then we must be free from the bondage of addiction, whatever form it takes. This is not to discount the very real struggle that comes with addiction to pornography, gambling, or other vices, or the physical symptoms of withdrawal from drugs or alcohol, but rather to recognize that breaking free from any addiction requires both physical and spiritual effort.

Venerable Matthew Talbot was an alcoholic. Liquor was his compulsion of choice, but the lessons we can learn from his life are applicable to all addictions, even those that society says are "acceptable." His example of how he faced and dealt with his addiction—and the suffering that it brought into his life—shows us how we can deal with any compulsion or habit that keeps us from being completely free to serve God and others.

Matt Talbot was born into poverty in Dublin's inner city. He began drinking at the age of twelve and became an alcoholic soon afterward. After sixteen years of heavy drinking, he "took the pledge" to stop drinking for three months. After three months, he extended it to six, and eventually, with the help of a priest friend, his sobriety became lifelong, although he wrote to his sister, "Never look down on a man who cannot give up the drink. It is easier to get out of hell!" For forty years he struggled, although to his family and friends he seemed to be an ordinary hardworking man whose only "oddities" might have been his propensity to give most of his money to the poor, to live in sparse surroundings, and to attend Mass frequently. He was on his way to Mass, in fact, when he died of heart failure.

Even though his sobriety predated the precepts of Alcoholics Anonymous by several years, Matt Talbot's program incorporated many of the same principles, including reparation, self-discipline, spiritual reading, and hard work. If we are to battle our compulsions and free ourselves from the suffering caused by them, we would do well to follow his example.

Forgiveness and Reparation

One of the first things Matt did after giving up alcohol was to try to find a street musician whose fiddle he had stolen to buy a drink. When he was unable to locate the man so that he could reimburse him, he gave the money to the church to have Masses said. Since it is inevitable that our addictions are going to cause pain to someone (there is no such thing as a victimless addiction, even if we appear to be the only victim), then when we are serious about ending our addiction, we must make reparation to those we have hurt. We cannot heal until we have forgiven ourselves and those we have injured. If it's not possible to ask forgiveness from others, then like Matt, we need to find some other way to make amends. If we do not seek forgiveness, then the suffering that we experience from our addictive tendencies, even if we stop the actual behavior, will continue to fester. This is true, not just of the suffering from addiction, but from all suffering that stems from our own choices. Making reparation is an essential first step as we turn from self-destruction to hope, from blame to accountability.

Pope Benedict XVI made this point when he spoke to a group of young addicts in Australia:

> A vivid illustration of what it means to turn back from the path of death onto the path of life is found in a Gospel story that I am sure you all know well: the parable of the prodigal son. When that young man left his father's house at the beginning of the story, he was seeking the illusory pleasures promised by false "gods." He squandered his inheritance on a life of indulgence, and ended up in abject poverty and misery. When he reached the very lowest point, hungry and abandoned, he realized how foolish he had been to leave his loving father. Humbly, he returned and asked forgiveness. Joyfully, his father embraced him and exclaimed: "This son of mine was dead, and has come back to life; he was lost, and is found" (Luke 15:24).[1]

A second lesson we can learn from Matt Talbot's life and example is that we need to exercise self-discipline. Of course, we all know that self-discipline isn't much fun. It certainly isn't as much fun as whatever behavior we're addicted to, and let's be honest, most addictions start out with an element of pleasure, fun, or excitement, or otherwise we would not continue doing them long enough to become addicted. It's only later, when the pain becomes greater than the pleasure, that most of us are willing to change. Pope Benedict acknowledged this when he spoke to the Australians.

> Perhaps you have made choices that you now regret, choices that led you down a path which, however attractive it appeared at the time, only led you deeper into misery and abandonment. The choice to abuse drugs or alcohol, to engage in criminal activity or self-harm, may have seemed at the time to offer a way out of a difficult or confusing situation. You now know that, instead of bringing life, it brings death.[2]

Like all addicts, Matt Talbot had to exercise self-discipline in order not to take up drinking again, but he did more than just resist the urge to drink. Some of his additional self-discipline came in the form of physical mortification—he slept on a hard plank, ate very little, and even wore chains about his waist, arm, and leg (a form of physical discipline that had been recommended by his spiritual advisor). He also maintained a cheerful attitude at all times, obeying his employers and putting in an honest day's labor for a day's wages. Most of us aren't going to follow his example of wrapping chains about our limbs, but we can emulate his self-discipline by controlling our attitude, working diligently at our occupations, and putting the needs of others before our own desires.

Why is self-discipline important when dealing with the suffering associated with addiction? As is the case with so many other kinds of suffering, it's because living a disciplined life stops the cycle of self-pity. When we aren't thinking about ourselves and our desires, we are far less likely to wallow in our pain. Often whatever we concentrate on intensifies, so if want to lessen our suffering, we must stop focusing on it. Living a disciplined life is the key to making that happen.

DAILY SPIRITUAL READING

A third lesson from Matt Talbot's life is the importance of incorporating regular spiritual reading and spiritual practices into our lives. With two thousand years of history, the Catholic Church has ample spiritual reading material in its treasure troves, from the early Church fathers to the pope's current best sellers, not to mention the Bible itself. Spending even ten minutes a day, either in the morning or before bedtime, to read something that is uplifting and edifying can give you an added boost of resolve to face the challenges that come with battling addictions.

We don't have to be limited to "church" material either. One of my all-time favorite books is *Simple Abundance*. The author, Sarah Ban Breathnach, gently reminds us of the importance of truly living in the present each and every day. Another favorite of mine is *The Artist's Way* by Julia Cameron, which contains practical ideas for starting and maintaining the creative process (and since God is the ultimate creator and we are made in God's image, developing our creativity is a Spirit-inspired endeavor!). Neither of these books is overtly religious, but both contain spiritual wisdom that has helped me through some rough spots in my life. Give yourself permission to find something that truly speaks to your soul, and then read it daily.

Along with reading (mostly the Scriptures), Matt Talbot also incorporated traditional practices of the Church, such as saying the Rosary, into his everyday life. We, too, need to find spiritual practices that nourish our being, and then we need to do them, if not daily, at least frequently. If we find the devotions that Matt did to be helpful, we should do them, but if not, we need to find something else that suits us. I find going to an adoration chapel and sitting in the silence to be deeply restorative. I've also walked a modified labyrinth I have in my backyard, done centering prayer, and meditated in a small prayer corner in my house.

One of the best spiritual practices, both in terms of self-discipline and spiritual growth, is daily Mass, something Matt Talbot did for more than forty years. However, that may not be feasible for many of us; some parishes don't offer daily Mass, or if they do, it may be held at a time when we can't attend. If that's the case with you, yet you feel drawn toward daily Mass, then praying through the Mass readings from the Scriptures each day or even using the daily Roman Missal may be a beneficial practice. You may also want to try praying the Liturgy of the Hours, the official public prayer of the Church, at the various times prescribed during the day and night.

Whatever you choose, make sure you actually make a choice—and not just think about doing something sometime in the future. As Matt Talbot shows us, it's the "daily-ness" of our actions that helps us overcome the suffering that we bring into our lives through addictions. In the words of the last homily of another recovering alcoholic, Fr. Mychal Judge, who was among the first to die on 9/11: "Good days. And bad days. Up days. Down days. Sad days. Happy days. . . . You do what God has called you to do. You show up. You put one foot in front of another. . . . He needs you. He needs me. He needs all of us."[3]

Spiritual reading and spiritual discipline are two of the best ways we have of "showing up" and "putting one foot in front of the other." We need them both if we are to become liberated from our suffering.

THE BLESSINGS OF PHYSICAL LABOR

Finally, Matt Talbot leaves us one final lesson for dealing with the pain of our addictions: physical labor. When we move our bodies, exercise our muscles, and break a sweat, chemical changes occur within our cells. As humans, we were created to move, and movement makes us feel better mentally and physically. When we feel better, we are able to make wiser decisions, exercise greater self-control and self-discipline, and cope with suffering without resorting to self-destructive behaviors.

Matt was a laborer, a hod carrier, and a construction worker for all of his adult life, and is remembered for taking on the hardest and dirtiest jobs without complaint. In following his example, we aren't obliged to become manual laborers (I would be fired the first hour, if I lasted that long!). But we all have opportunities in our ordinary lives to do something physical—for example, scrubbing the toilet, washing the dishes, mowing the lawn, or vacuuming the floors. When we feel the pain returning or the temptations creeping in, "getting physical" can be one of the best and fastest ways to regain our equilibrium and peace of mind.

The pain of being held in bondage to something that seems outside of our control is common to most of us, even those of us who have never battled "classic" addictions. As we struggle against something even as seemingly innocent as the compulsion to check our e-mail every hour or a desire for an extra-large cola each afternoon, we can take heart that our struggles break open our hearts to accept God's love. As Pope Benedict reminds us:

All through the Gospels, it was those who had taken wrong turnings who were particularly loved by Jesus, because once they recognized their mistake, they were all the more open to his healing message. . . . It was those who were willing to rebuild their lives that were most ready to listen to Jesus and become his disciples. You can follow in their footsteps; you, too, can grow particularly close to Jesus because you have chosen to turn back toward him. You can be sure that, just like the Father in the story of the prodigal son, Jesus welcomes you with open arms. He offers you unconditional love—and it is in loving friendship with him that the fullness of life is to be found.[4]

FOR CONSIDERATION

1. In what ways am I not fully free in my life? What compulsions, habits, or addictions are enslaving me?

2. Have I talked to God about this issue in prayer? Am I ready and willing to surrender to God whatever is enslaving me?

3. If I am addicted to a substance like alcohol or drugs, what steps have I taken toward recovery? Have I asked forgiveness for those who have been injured by my behavior? Have I confessed my sin, forgiven myself for my bad choices, and made a firm resolve to change?

4. What spiritual practices are part of my daily life? Are they bearing fruit? What other practices might I want to consider?

5. In what ways do I live a disciplined life? In what ways do I need more discipline? What would help me to exercise more discipline? Could someone help me to be accountable?

6. How often do I engage in physical "labor," even if it's only exercise? How has it helped me in combating the temptations of addiction or compulsions?

7. Do I engage in regular spiritual reading? What has been most helpful to me? How can I expand my choices and incorporate such reading into my daily life?

Prayer
AGAINST TEMPTATION

Venerable Matt Talbot, God has said to us that he will not let us be tempted beyond what we can bear. May I always remember that promise, trusting that God is indeed faithful to his word. Through your intercession, help me to recognize that when I am tempted, God will always provide a way out so that I can stand up under the temptation. Be with me as I struggle today so that, like you, I may have the courage to take up my cross and follow daily in the footsteps of our Lord and Savior. Amen. (Based on 1 Corinthians 10:13)

— Chapter 6 —

Divorce

St. Helena

She grew up in the bawdy atmosphere of her father's tavern, probably assuming that she would marry one of the tradesmen or military personnel who were barracked nearby. She certainly never expected anything more than the hardscrabble life of her parents and their parents before them. Then one day a handsome young officer entered the bar and asked for a drink. The girl fell head over heels in love, as did the young man. They soon set up housekeeping, and he quickly rose through the ranks of the army to become a general. They probably got married sometime before their son was born, but it was a small private affair, at best. He continued his upwardly mobile career until he literally reached the top rank of government.

One devastating day, the woman, who was no longer young and beautiful, learned that her husband had begun an affair with a younger woman who had better social connections. Within a few months, he married his mistress, this time with all the pomp, circumstances, and fancy trappings of a "real" wedding. The mother of his son was left to fend for herself, a middle-aged woman with no education, no prospects, and no future.

This story sounds like something from the pages of a contemporary novel, but her story is nearly two thousand years old. She is Flavia Iulia Helena Augusta, mother of the emperor Constantine. We know her as St. Helena (ca. 250–330).

St. Helena should be the patron saint of the First Wives' Club, and indeed, she is the patron of those who are divorced. How she handled her life after Emperor Flavious Valerius Constantius left her to marry Theodora, the stepdaughter of his co-emperor, Maximian, is nothing less than inspiring, even after all these years.

But back to her story. While the date of her conversion from the state religion of Rome to Christianity is unknown, it undoubtedly happened after her son, Constantine, became the first Christian Roman emperor. Her conversion became the fulcrum for her life after divorce. One of the Church fathers, Eusebius, wrote that under Constantine's influence, Helena became "such a devout servant of God, that one might believe her to have been from her very childhood a disciple of the Redeemer of mankind." She built churches and, by all accounts, led an exemplary life of sacrifice and prayer. In her seventies she undertook a pilgrimage to Palestine where, according to tradition, she found the relics of Jesus' cross. She continued her work on behalf of the poor until her death at the age of eighty.

Even though she lived nearly twenty centuries ago, St. Helena's life provides practical advice on how to deal with the pain that comes from separation, loss of love, and divorce.

One of the most important things her life teaches us is that divorce itself is not a barrier to sanctity. Because the Catholic Church teaches that marriage is irrevocable and that divorce is one of the great ills of modern society, people sometimes get the mistaken idea that divorce is a sin in and of itself and therefore an impediment to holiness. It isn't, as Helena and other divorced saints such as Fabiola and Guntramnus show us. However, one of the reasons that this mistaken belief arose was because until recent years, divorce was so rare among Christians. Christians just didn't get divorced, period. Those who did were ostracized, not just by the Church, but by society in general. Even as late as the 1930s and 40s, a reference to a "divorced woman" could be a thinly veiled euphemism for a woman of less than sterling reputation.

Another reason divorce has been seen as an impediment to holiness is because the Church has always forbidden divorce and remarriage without an annulment. In the absence of an annulment, a couple remains bound to each other in the eyes of the Church, and remarriage in that case constitutes adultery, which is a serious sin. As the *Catechism of the Catholic Church* teaches:

> Divorce does injury to the covenant of salvation, of which sacramental marriage is the sign. Contracting a new union, even if it is recognized by civil law, adds to the gravity of the rupture: the remarried spouse is then in a situation of public and permanent adultery. . . .
>
> Divorce is immoral also because it introduces disorder into the family and into society. This disorder brings grave harm to the deserted spouse, to children traumatized by the separation of their parents and often torn between them, and because of its contagious effect which makes it truly a plague on society. (2384, 2385)

However, the *Catechism* goes on to say, in accord with long-established tradition:

It can happen that one of the spouses is the innocent victim of a divorce decreed by civil law; this spouse therefore has not contravened the moral law. There is a considerable difference between a spouse who has sincerely tried to be faithful to the sacrament of marriage and is unjustly abandoned, and one who through his own grave fault destroys a canonically valid marriage. (2386)

Such was the case with Helena and is often the case with many who are divorced. Even if a person initiates a divorce, as long as no remarriage is attempted, he or she remains in good standing with the Church and may still receive all the sacraments, including the Eucharist. The fact is that merely being divorced does not mean one can't be holy or even saintly. It's what one does after a divorce that counts.

DON'T LINGER IN THE PAIN

Another valuable lesson that we can learn from Helena is that when it comes to divorce, pain is probable, but a lifetime of suffering is optional. What does that mean? It means that it will hurt when a relationship ends. Emotionally, financially, spiritually, and perhaps even physically, divorce is painful. Helena's life was shattered when the emperor divorced her. She didn't even have a good divorce attorney to get a settlement! She was literally tossed out of the palace onto the street. The pain, not to mention the worry and fear, could have been crippling. However, Helena didn't let her pain morph into a lifetime of suffering. That's the difference. Continuing to linger in the hurt, continuing to pick at the scab to keep the wound raw, continuing to focus on the ache to the exclusion of the rest of life—that's what creates a lifetime of suffering out of an undeniably painful event. It's not something that God is allowing in our lives; it's something we are doing to ourselves. We are perpetuating our suffering out of a painful situation by our own choices.

Instead of becoming mired in her pain, Helena did what virtually all the saints do when confronted with adversity: She got busy. She aided the poor, convinced her son to finance the building of churches, organized pilgrimages, and generally lived life when she could easily have just waited around to die. She probably still felt a few stabs of pain when she saw Theodora on the arms of her former spouse, but by keeping herself busy, she was able to move on with grace.

When my own marriage ended, I was deeply saddened, and I still am when I think of all that could have been. However, like Helena, I have found that activity, both physical and mental, is the best antidote to the creeping cancer of regret and anger. Now, most of us aren't going to literally build churches, as Helena did, but we can build God's kingdom by offering our time and service in any number of worthy causes. If you find yourself slipping into a pattern of unrelenting pain and suffering after a separation or a divorce, get up and do something. What you do isn't as important as the fact that you are getting out of the trap of self-pity as quickly as possible. Because of Helena's age (she was considered quite elderly at a time when thirty was thought of as middle-aged), she didn't have any time to waste. But no matter what our age, we shouldn't squander any of our valuable days either. It's okay to feel the pain, experience the grief, express the anger . . . but don't allow yourself to get stuck in these emotions Remember, God is pained along with you by divorce. He is not going to love you more if you try to add more pain to the situation!

Another way Helena can be an example to those who suffer from divorce is not to create hard feelings between the children and the other parent. We can't be sure exactly how Helena dealt with her "ex" in regard to their son, but since her son succeeded his father as emperor and at the same time remained supportive of his mother and her endeavors (including funding her expedition to the Holy Land), we can extrapolate that Helena must not have tried to sow bitterness between them. It's tempting to try to get your children to take your "side" in a divorce, but that is guaranteed to create suffering that could be prevented for you and for them. Remember that no matter what happened in your marital relationship, your former spouse is still your child's parent. If the situation were truly one-sided (and it rarely is), as your children grow up, they will begin to see the reality. Even if they never see your perspective on the reason for the breakup, attempting to get them to think badly of the other parent is doomed to backfire. Take the high road; you will suffer much less in the long run.

NEW BEGINNINGS

Yet another example we can derive from the life of St. Helena is to let the past be past. Helena went from being a nothing in a tavern to being the empress, then down to nothing again, and then back into favor when her son assumed the throne. Throughout her life, she continually moved forward and "reinvented" herself, most notably in her last years as an archaeologist! The story goes that on her trip to the Holy Land, she tore down a temple to Venus that had been built on the site of Jesus' tomb. Finding three crosses beneath the rubble, she asked a terminally ill woman to touch each of them. When the woman laid her hand on the third cross, she was miraculously healed, and Helena pronounced the wood as coming from the cross of Christ. She is also said to have found the nails that were used to crucify Jesus, and she was instrumental in establishing the first Church of the Holy Sepulcher in Jerusalem, the site of Jesus' tomb and resurrection. Now, it might be fanciful to imagine Helena wielding a shovel as she searched for evidence of the crucifixion, but she did travel thousands of miles on foot and horseback to a hostile and foreign land at a time when women didn't travel, much less in old age. And it is a historical fact that she brought back excavated relics that were traditionally believed to be the true cross.

That archaeological expedition shows us that divorce need not be an impediment to living a rewarding life. In fact, if we believe the promise that "all things work together for good for those who love God" (Romans 8:28), out of the pain of divorce may come an unexpected freedom to fulfill a lifelong mission that we had put on hold. "Every cloud has a silver lining" is a cliché, but clichés often contain some truth. When we look for the lesson that our suffering from divorce might be teaching us, we may just discover that proverbial silver lining. Is there something you have always felt called to do but have ignored because at the time, you rightfully put the needs of your spouse first? Is there a dream you had put off because marriage took you down a different path? Helena shows us that if we are willing to look beyond our immediate pain, we may just find a new beginning. Perhaps the unexpected blessing hidden in the pain of divorce is a second chance at life.

The final lesson Helena gives us is that if we are to move beyond the suffering of a divorce or separation, we need to fill the emptiness we are going to experience with positive, creative, life-enhancing relationships. This is actually good advice for any kind of suffering, but it's particularly relevant for the pain that follows divorce. It's all too easy to become withdrawn and isolated since friendships inevitably change, finances are affected, and family members often react with blame and hostility. However, when we isolate ourselves, the temptation grows to attempt to dull our ache with food, drugs, the Internet, or any number of addictive behaviors, which in turn create more suffering. So even when it seems the most difficult, we need to use Helena as an example and move on through the pain of the loss of marriage into whatever life and new relationships still await us.

It may seem odd that the patron of divorced persons dates back almost to the beginning of Christianity, but it is also comforting to realize that no matter what kind of suffering we may experience, a saint has been there before us. In fact, Helena might never have become a saint if she hadn't been divorced, since her conversion and her good works began only after she was no longer married. Interesting thought, isn't it?

FOR CONSIDERATION

1. How do I view divorce? Do I judge those who are divorced and assume it is their fault? How can I reach out to those whose marriages have broken up?

2. Am I able to move forward in my life after a loss, whatever that may be, rather than focusing on my pain? What activities might help me to do so?

3. If I have suffered a marriage breakup or separation, am I judging myself more harshly than God does over my divorce or separation? Do I still see my life as a path to holiness? Why or why not?

4. If I am now recently divorced or widowed, how can I use my new situation in a creative way? In what way am I being given a second chance because of divorce or the loss of a spouse through death to do things I didn't have the opportunity to do previously?

5. Have I taken responsibility for whatever role I might have played in a divorce? Have I asked for forgiveness? Have I forgiven myself?

6. If I am divorced with children, how have I dealt with relating to my ex-spouse? Have I ever been tempted to control my children's relationship with their other parent in order to make myself feel better?

7. How often do I struggle with self-pity? What might I do when self-pity strikes?

8. In what ways might I be clinging to the past? What might help me to let go and look forward to what God might have in mind for my life now?

9. Can I trust that God is with me as I move on to the next stage of my life? Can I trust that he will guide me?

Prayer
OF A DIVORCED OR SEPARATED PERSON

Father, I belong to you.
I place myself anew in your hands
and acknowledge you as Master and Lord of my life.
Grant me the gift of a forgiving heart
and cleanse me of any anger,
hostility, or revenge.
Heal my hurts and wounds and teach me to rely on your love.
Grant me wisdom of heart
and strengthen me by your grace to move on in faith,
in trust and in love.
Thank you, Lord, for your love in my life. Amen.[1]

— CHAPTER 7 —

Life Choices

St. Margaret of Cortona and

St. Damien de Veuster

We all know that we can create suffering from the choices we make in life. Often we tend to believe that such suffering is always the result of inopportune, foolish, or even bad choices—the girl who becomes pregnant out of wedlock, the couple whose marriage fails because of adultery, the gambler who loses everything because of his addiction. But not all suffering from the life choices we make is a result of poor decisions. Sometimes adversity occurs because we were fully intending to fulfill our God-given purpose in life when we made our choice, and it just happens that our decision carries consequences that lead to our suffering. In this chapter we will look at both sides of the suffering that comes from our choices: the bad, as shown in the life of St. Margaret of Cortona (1247–February 22, 1297), and the good, as in the life of St. Damien of Molokai (January 3, 1840–April 15, 1889).

The story of Margaret of Cortona reads like something out of a supermarket tabloid. Her mother died when she was seven. She and her stepmother never got along, so at seventeen she ran away to live with her boyfriend, Arsenio. They had a son, and while Arsenio kept promising for ten years to marry her, he never quite got around to it. One day when he failed to return from a trip,

Margaret followed his favorite hunting hound into the forest and found his body, which his murderers had left in a shallow grave.

Margaret tried to return to her father's home, but her step-mother wasn't amenable to having an unwed mother under her roof, so Margaret and her son ended up being taken care of by the friars of Cortona. Eventually she became a Franciscan tertiary and helped found a hospital for the homeless and impoverished, living the rest of her life in ways befitting a saint.

Clearly, virtually all of Margaret's pain and suffering—being rejected by her family for her lifestyle, becoming a single mom, living in poverty—are the consequences of her own choices (although her stepmother's lack of charity didn't help matters). So what does Margaret's life teach us about suffering from our ill-conceived life choices? First and probably foremost, it shows us that we need to think carefully about the consequences of our actions. What might seem like a momentary good thing— getting away from a harsh stepmother by living with someone who loves us—can have long-term costs. To be fair, often people make these kinds of decisions when they are young, vulnerable, and naïve. Unfortunately, those who have escaped making bad decisions can sometimes fall into the trap of being judgmental of others who were not so strong or fortunate. Even Margaret recognized this, saying, "I see more Pharisees among Christians than there were around Pilate."

REFRAIN FROM JUDGMENT

Which brings us to a second lesson from her life: Don't judge either the reasons for another person's suffering or the path that led them to their pain. Remember that Jesus said, "Do not judge, so that you may not be judged" (Matthew 7:1). We might be able to see how a rash decision has led to another's suffering, but we have no right to pass judgment on what brought the person to make that choice, and specifically, we have no right to decide the relative sinfulness of the action. On the surface, it would appear that Margaret's decision to live with her boyfriend and bear him a child without marriage would be a grave sin, but we don't—and can't—know the exact state of Margaret's conscience at the time. We simply can't become another's moral judge and jury based merely on what we observe.

Conversely, if we are the ones who made the bad choices, constantly beating ourselves up for those decisions isn't constructive either. We need to forgive ourselves, make whatever amends we can, and get on with our lives. It may be hard to believe, especially if we have been raised with the heavy hand of guilt resting on our heads, but God doesn't really want us to suffer from guilt. Guilt is a gift that helps us to perceive our mistakes and sin, but God wants us to learn from those bad choices and then let go of the guilt. Clinging to guilt doesn't make us better people, and it doesn't make God love us more.

One last thing we can draw from Margaret's life is that God really can use all things for good. Margaret's choices led her to suffering, but they also led her to sanctity. It is said that when Margaret was at prayer, she heard our Lord say:

My child, think on the manifold graces and lights with which I have endowed thy soul, in order to turn thee to Me. Think of how, on the death of the enemy of your salvation, overcome with sorrow, with downcast looks, bathed in tears, and clothed in black, you came in confusion to Laviano, to your father's house. Think of how, at the instigation of your stepmother, he altogether forgot fatherly compassion, and drove you from the house. Deprived of human advice and aid, you knew not what to do; you withdrew into the garden, and sat beneath a fig tree, and wept. You turned toward me, beseeching me to be your master, your father, your spouse, your Lord; and you humbly deplored your spiritual and corporal misery.[1]

When we find ourselves suffering because of some wrong road we've taken, the single most important thing we can do is to ask what lesson we can learn from our suffering—and then pray to have the courage to act upon that lesson for our future good. It's what Margaret and, indeed, virtually all the saints have done and what we must do as well if we are to use our suffering as a means of growth and not merely as something to be endured.

But there is another side to the pain that comes from our choices in life, and that's the suffering that goes along with a good, even holy decision. Most of us intuitively understand this kind of pain—ask any parent. The decision to have children is an honorable one, but along with that choice will undoubtedly come some suffering, for love is always claw-marked with pain. As the great British apologist C. S. Lewis wrote:

To love at all is to be vulnerable. Love anything, and your heart will certainly be wrung and possibly broken. If you want to make sure of keeping it intact, you must give your heart to no one, not even to an animal. Wrap it carefully round with hobbies and little luxuries; avoid all entanglements; lock it up safe in the casket or coffin of your selfishness. But in that casket—safe, dark, motionless, airless—it will change. It will not be broken; it will become unbreakable, impenetrable, irredeemable.[2]

The fact is that often when we make a choice out of love, we inadvertently also end up being handed suffering as well. St. Damien of Molokai is a fitting example of a modern-day saint whose decision to love resulted in his own personal pain.

Along with his brother, Auguste, Damien became a Picpus brother and eventually was ordained a priest. He longed to be a missionary, but his brother was selected to go to Hawaii instead of him. When Auguste fell ill, Damien took his place. Upon his arrival, the bishop asked for volunteers to work with people who had contracted leprosy. Since leprosy was thought to be both fatal and highly contagious, such an assignment was considered a death sentence. Fr. Damien was the first to volunteer. He lived and worked among the lepers at the remote and isolated colony on Molokai for more than twenty years, until his own death from leprosy.

Thinking Through Our Decisions

St. Damien's life, like Margaret's, exemplifies the need to think seriously about our choices and be willing to live with the consequences. Remember, all decisions have natural consequences, and generally speaking, God allows us to experience them. We can always ask that suffering be removed, but it is uncommon for God to remove suffering from choices that we have made deliberately. When we choose a life course that entails suffering along the way, we are undoubtedly going to experience that suffering. Think of it this way: If we plant beets, we don't expect God to miraculously produce carrots.

Fr. Damien knew that if he went to Molokai, he could contract Hansen's disease. He chose to go anyway. When he spilled boiling water on his foot without experiencing pain and realized that he had become infected, he was neither surprised nor angry. He had already accepted whatever suffering might result from his original decision to work among the lepers. In fact, he said, "Having no doubts about the true nature of the disease, I am calm, resigned, and very happy in the midst of my people. God certainly knows what is best for my sanctification and I gladly repeat: 'Thy will be done.'"[3]

Fr. Damien's life teaches us once again that we must be prudent when we enter into something that carries a potentially high price. Just because the price is steep, however, doesn't mean that we shouldn't do it. On the contrary, it might be exactly what our life's mission is, what we were created to do. In the case of Fr. Damien, his life brought to light the plight of lepers and was a contributing factor in finding a cure for Hansen's disease. One could say that he had been created to work with lepers. However, he also understood all too well the price that he would end up paying. Perhaps the greatest lesson that Damien teaches us is that once we make a choice to follow what we believe is our purpose in life, even if it will undoubtedly cause us suffering, we have to be willing to see it through.

That doesn't mean, however, that we feel the emotion of joy at every moment (if that were even possible!). We can always take our struggles to God, even the struggles that come from our own choices. As Damien said:

> Jesus in the Blessed Sacrament is the most tender of friends with souls who seek to please Him. His goodness knows how to proportion itself to the smallest of His creatures as to the greatest of them. Be not afraid then in your solitary conversations, to tell Him of your miseries, your fears, your worries, of those who are dear to you, of your projects, and of your hopes. Do so with confidence and with an open heart.[4]

Another important aspect of the lessons we can learn from Fr. Damien is that our choice to willingly accept consequences can have transformative effects, not only on the people in our immediate vicinity, but throughout time and space. Consider for a moment that Fr. Damien's statue stands in the Hall of Statues in Washington, D.C. He is one of six Catholics so honored, and the only canonized saint. (The other five are Fr. Jacques Marquette, Fr. Eusebio Kino, Fr. Junipero Serra, Mother Joseph of the Sisters of Providence, and Charles Carroll of Maryland, the only Catholic who signed the Declaration of Independence.) Even those who do not share Damien's Catholic faith or even the Christian faith are inspired by his example of self-sacrifice and self-giving. In fact, Mahatma Gandhi claimed that Fr. Damien was one of his models for social change in India. He is quoted in M. S. Mehendale's 1971 account, *Gandhi Looks at Leprosy*, as saying, "The political and journalistic world can boast of very few heroes who compare with Father Damien of Molokai. It is worthwhile to look for the sources of such heroism."

DON'T ASSUME THE WORST

Another lesson we can learn from Damien concerns the danger of making unwarranted assumptions. If Damien had assumed that he would contract leprosy as soon as he arrived on the island and began to interact with the people, he may have been worried about it the whole time, even though it didn't happen until years later. Such a state of mind would surely have hurt his work among the people. The truth is that making the wrong assumptions is the source of much unnecessary suffering. That's because when we assume, we generally assume the worst-case scenario, and when we assume the worst, we almost guarantee that we are going to suffer. For example, your child is a few minutes late getting home from school. If you assume that your child has met with an accident or a predator, you will suffer intently those few minutes until he or she arrives, when all that actually happened was that he or she talked a bit too long after school. The suffering that comes from assuming the worst is almost always unnecessary; it's not suffering that God wants us to have.

Of course, we might be tempted to assume that it was easier for Damien to face getting leprosy than it would be for us, but that might be another wrong assumption. Saints do difficult things that we might not attempt, not because they find them easier than we would, but because they are able to see a greater picture. Damien was able to look beyond his own life to see what could be done to help alleviate the suffering of others and to bring others to Christ. Because of that, he was able to face the possibility of disease with courage instead of panic.

Finally, the lives of both St. Damien and St. Margaret teach us that we should not waste time second-guessing our decisions. If Damien had second-guessed his original decision about taking his brother's place as a missionary, he might never have fulfilled his true calling. But what about second-guessing a bad decision? Revisiting a choice and regretting our decisions are part of being human. Margaret of Cortona deeply regretted her choices and performed years of penance for them. However, getting stuck in regret means that we haven't learned from our choices and that we aren't moving forward. Living with regret is simply another way of perpetuating suffering that God never intended for us. Peace comes when we accept that we've made a decision—be it good or bad—and go on with our lives. In the end, it isn't so much what we have chosen but what we have chosen *to do* with our choices that makes the difference.

FOR CONSIDERATION

1. As I reflect on my life, what are some major choices I have made, and where did they lead me? How can I see God's hand in my choices, good or bad?

2. How often do I beat myself up for past bad decisions? If this is a pattern in my life, what would help me to move away from it? How could a spiritual counselor or trusted friend help me?

3. How often do I pray and ask for guidance before making a decision that may have long-term consequences? If I have done so in the past, how has this helped me?

4. What lessons might I be able to learn from the choices I've made in my life that I've come to regret? Is there something I can give thanks for even in the midst of my pain?

5. Is there a "silver lining" that has come from a bad choice? How has this blessed me or my loved ones?

6. If I have made a decision that is part of my God-given purpose in life, do I also believe that I will be given the strength and courage to see it through?

7. How often do I complain about suffering that comes from following a vocation or calling that I know is God's will for my life? What would help me to better deal with this pain?

8. What unnecessary suffering have I created for myself by making assumptions that turn out not to be the case? How can I move away from this type of thinking?

9. If I am stuck in pain because I refuse to move out of regret, have I been willing to let go of that pain? What might help me to let go? How would prayer and the sacraments help?

Prayer

TO ST. DAMIEN

Oh St. Damien, enlightened by the Holy Spirit and moved by the sorrows of the poor, you dedicated yourself tirelessly to the service of the lepers and became one like them. In doing so, you enhanced their God-given dignity to the last minutes of your priestly life, regardless of many trials and sufferings. Since then, your name has become a great inspiration for countless people throughout the world.

We, touched by your self-sacrifice, beseech you to help us follow in your footsteps in sharing our time, energy, talents, and other God-endowed gifts with our brothers and sisters in the Lord. Now you have been glorified with Jesus Christ in the Heavenly Kingdom. We ask you to continue interceding for us before our loving and caring God, that we may have the gift of faith in Him, humility, and the courage to bring love and healing to our poor brothers and sisters in the world.[5]

— CHAPTER 8 —

Marital Discord

ST. RITA OF CASCIA AND

ST. CATHERINE OF GENOA

W e tend to think that marital discord is a contemporary problem, that somehow people of earlier generations (with a few notable exceptions like Henry VIII) married well and lived happily ever after. That assumption extends to the saints. Since the vast majority of saints weren't married, the myth persists that the relatively few married saints that we know about must have had happy, blessed marriages.

The reality is another story. Happily married saints who actually remained together throughout their lives and who didn't abandon their marriages in the mistaken belief that becoming a nun, monk, or priest was a higher calling are few and far between. Of the saints who did remain married until "death do us part," many saints had difficult, troubled, and even abusive marriages. In fact, twenty-five saints are listed as patrons for difficult marriages while only one (St. Valentine) is traditionally cited for happy marriages!

St. Rita of Cascia (1386–1456) may have had one of the worst marriages of all. Margherita, nicknamed "Rita," was the only child of Antonio and Amata Lotti, residents of the Italian republic of Cascia. Perhaps to insure her financial security, her parents married her off at the age of twelve to Paolo Mancini, the town

87

watchmaker. To say that Paolo was an unpleasant man is an understatement. Even by the lenient standards of his time, he was considered an abusive husband and father. Because early hagiographies shied away from dwelling on such unpleasant and unspiritual topics as spousal abuse, just the fact that all accounts of Rita's married life describe Paolo as "exceedingly cruel" and "ill-tempered" attest to the miserable marriage she endured. Despite the lack of precise details, even today, more than five hundred years after her death, the history of her bad marriage continues, as she is often cited as the patron of battered wives.

Rita's life and marriage afford us several lessons about adversity, but they might not be the ones you would expect. Yes, we might learn patience and endurance from her example, since she lived with Paolo for eighteen years until he was murdered by a rival family faction. However, it's not clear that Rita patiently put up with her ill-treatment because it allowed her to offer it up for the greater glory of God; she may simply have had no other option. Even after Paolo's death, when she attempted to enter the local Augustinian convent, the nuns initially refused to accept her because the familial rivalries that plagued that region ran deep even in the convent. So it's entirely feasible that Rita might have made a choice other than remaining under Paolo's thumb if she had been afforded the opportunity.

Another possible lesson we might expect to learn from her is how to endure marital discord in prayerful silence. Again, while prayerful silence can be virtuous, this isn't something we can automatically extrapolate from Rita's life. It's true that Rita prayed, but we have no idea if she was a blissful saint, as she is often pictured on holy cards, or if she was feisty and outspoken—traits that might have actually resulted in greater mistreatment from Paolo. We simply don't have enough historical evidence to know if she reacted to her marital suffering in silence or not.

So what can we learn from her life and example?

One of the first lessons is not to blame other family members for the problems in our own marriage. Many times our families do and say things that are painful or create additional hardships in our relationship with our spouses, but blaming them (even when it is justifiable) does nothing to modify the situation. It would have been very easy (and even legitimate) for Rita to have blamed her parents for marrying her off at a young age to such a dreadful man. But there is no evidence that Rita ever did or said anything against her family. In fact, later in life, she was known for brokering a peace treaty with the family of her husband's murderers, and her own parents were actually called "peacemakers." So it seems fairly safe to assume that Rita wasn't speaking out against her own family about the problems she had with Paolo. She may have said something to them in private, but it's unlikely she did so in public.

Now, there would have been practical reasons for this. Given the time and culture, it would have done no good for Rita to berate her parents. They couldn't change things, and complaining about Paolo probably would have made him even more abusive. But even in our own day, there is a lesson we can take from Rita: Our marriage is *our* marriage. What happens within it belongs to us, not to our families. While it's not healthy to mutely and secretly accept abuse, neither is it beneficial to try to shift the blame for marital unhappiness onto other family members. An unhappy marriage is primarily the responsibility of the husband and wife, not that of parents, brothers, sisters, in-laws, or friends.

Accept Reality but Don't Settle

A second corollary lesson from Rita's marriage is that sometimes we just have to accept reality. We don't have to like it, but before we can change things, we may have to simply accept them for what they are. We are born to certain parents. We live in a certain area. We come from a certain ethnic background. We have a certain type of childhood. We marry a certain person. We can't change our past, so we need to make peace with it before we can move on. It seems that's just what Rita did; she accepted the fact that her parents had made an unwise choice in selecting Paolo for her husband. In the words of St. Catherine of Genoa (1447–September 15, 1510), another saint whose parents arranged a bad marriage, "We must not wish anything other than what happens from moment to moment, all the while, however, exercising ourselves in goodness."

This leads us to another important lesson we can gain from the life of St. Rita in regard to an unhappy marriage: Accept, but don't settle. There's a big difference between accepting and settling. Settling means you give up, you don't care, and you may even teeter on the brink of despair. Settling means you become a victim. On the other hand, accepting means you recognize—and act upon—those things that are within your power and leave the rest in God's hands. In a difficult marriage, this might mean that you accept the reality of your spouse's temperament, but you don't settle for being battered; it may mean that you recognize that your spouse has a substance-abuse problem, but you don't settle for living in drug- and alcohol-created squalor. You get counseling, you find your own center, you cease thinking of yourself as a helpless victim of the situation. You acknowledge responsibility for your own life and choices and make whatever changes are necessary within you—not just to survive, but to find God's will and direction for your life and marriage.

Figuring this out isn't something most of us can do alone. We need divine assistance to sort out the difference between acceptance, which allows us to grow in holiness, and settling, which creates resentment and negativity. That's where Rita's example of prayer comes in. She might not have had a lot of options to change her life situation from the outside, but she knew—and used—the unlimited recourse she had on the inside through prayer.

Persistence in Prayer

We can't know for sure what Rita was praying for all the years that she was married to Paolo. She might have been praying that he would die, as he did, but she might also have been praying that he would change, or that she could enter a convent, or even that God might take her to heaven. Whatever it was that she was praying for, we know from the records that she prayed—and prayed persistently—for eighteen years until his death. (Incidentally, his demise must have brought her both relief and a little fear, especially since being widowed created its own set of problems in fifteenth-century Italy.)

Now, not all unhappy marriages will end with the death of one of the partners, but we can be assured that persistent prayer will have an effect on us, if not on our spouse. And once we change, we can be absolutely assured that our spouse will change too—hopefully for the better. Another patron of unhappy marriage shows us that truth in a profound way.

Giuliano Adorno, the husband of St. Catherine of Genoa, was violent, faithless, and financially irresponsible. Catherine spent the first five years of her marriage in sullen silence and the second five years finding pleasure wherever she could. Then she decided to spend three months praying to become bedridden to escape the marriage. When that didn't happen, she finally starting praying to know God's direction for her life. She soon came to realize that her life's mission was to care for the sick in the hospital at Genoa, so instead of fretting about her miserable marriage, she became involved in nursing. As a consequence, when she changed, so too did her husband. Eventually, Giuliano became a faithful and devout husband and a partner in her good works at the hospital.

Catherine's and Rita's persistence in the face of what must have seemed like ignored prayer brings us to an important question: Why must we sometimes persist so long before our prayers are answered? In the parables of the man who answers his door in the night because his neighbor keeps knocking (Luke 11:5-9) and the woman who harangued the unjust judge until she got her due (18:1-7), Jesus tells us that we should persevere in our petitions to God. But it can be puzzling as to why we seem to have to nag God to get an answer. One reason may be that persistence isn't so much for God as for us. We have to become very clear about what it is that we want. Persistence provides that laser focus. As we direct both our minds and emotions toward what it is that we want God to do for us, we simultaneously become increasingly aware of what it is that we really want and what we should be doing to help bring about that change. In that way prayer becomes not so much a series of requests that we send up like celestial e-mail but a cooperative effort in which God works with us to bring about the change and results we desire. This is particularly apparent in St. Catherine's life. She prayed to become sick, but she didn't really want to spend her life in bed; she wanted a better, happier, more fulfilling life. It was only after she became absolutely clear about what she wanted that her prayers were able to bring about the future she truly desired, including the change in her husband.

Rising Above the Pain

Finally, by looking at St. Rita's and St. Catherine's unhappy marriages and the suffering they endured, we can learn the importance of getting out of our own misery and focusing our time and attention on someone and something else. For St. Rita, it was her sons and her garden. She clearly was devoted to her boys and their highest good. The story is told that when they wanted to avenge their father's death by killing his murderers, she prayed that they would die before committing such a sin. Miracle or coincidence, they both fell fatally ill before they could carry out their plan. Now, we might not think that praying for the death of our children would be a good thing, but in Rita's time and culture, such an act would have been seen as a proactively positive move motivated by unselfish love. (We must always remember that saints lived in a specific time and place, and we cannot use our own cultural standards as the rod by which to measure their actions.) In addition to her sons, Rita was quite passionate about gardening, even asking that a rose and figs be brought from her garden in her hometown of Rocca Porrena when she was dying. Getting one's mind off the daily struggles of marital life by becoming lost in a creative hobby, such as gardening, is both healthy and holy. If St. Rita could do it, so can we.

For St. Catherine, it was only after her attention turned from her own life to caring for the sick in the hospital that she was able to rise above her pain. By discovering what she was good at and then following that calling, despite the suffering created by her marriage, she found the path to sanctity. And she clearly found her passion in the hospital, eventually becoming its treasurer and manager!

The suffering that comes from marital discord is one of the most difficult to endure, not the least because the Church teaches us that marriage is lifelong and permanent. But as St. Rita and St. Catherine show us, the pain that accompanies an unhappy marriage can become the crucible for discovering both our own strength as well as our life purpose, if we are willing to let it.

FOR CONSIDERATION

1. How often do I take an honest look to see what I may be doing to contribute to any unhappiness in my marital relationship?

2. Am I willing to take responsibility for my part in any discord in my marriage? Have I repented and tried to change?

3. When I pray about my marriage, do I ask that I change or that my spouse change? Why or why not?

4. Do I ever try to assign blame to someone outside the marriage for unhappiness within the marriage? How can I move beyond assigning blame?

5. What do I really want to happen in my marriage? Am I clear about my desires? Am I persistent in my prayer?

6. Do I accept the reality of my situation, or am I merely settling and enduring?

7. Do I have the courage to change myself, realizing that when I change, my spouse will change as well? What attitudes might be hindering me from being open to change?

8. Do I honestly believe that God wants what is best for both me and my spouse in our marriage?

Prayer
to St. Rita

St. Rita, come to my aid!
Faithful, loving wife and mother,
Humble, prayerful widow and nun,
Because of my need, answer my call.

St. Rita, come to my aid!
Beautiful rose born
from the Savior's thorns,
Lead me far from anger and hate;
Guide my heart on peaceful paths
with charity to all.

St. Rita, come to my aid!
Helper, healer, holy friend,
Hear my petition (make request).
To Christ take this prayer,
For He is my Lord, my God, my All,
My hope in despair,
My strength when afraid.

St. Rita, come to my aid!
St. Rita, answer my call. Amen.[1]

Chapter 9

Family Matters

St. Jane de Chantal

Since each of us comes into a relationship with a past and a history, which includes relatives, even the happiest of marriages can be troubled by the stress caused by other family members. Sometimes the pain from family members is created by our own parents interfering or meddling. For many, the pain is the result of having to deal with a mother-in-law or father-in-law, which is all the more difficult because we love our spouse and it is his or her parent who is the source of the discord and pain. Another way pain enters into families is through our children. While children are a delight and a blessing, every parent knows that along with the joy comes the inevitable pain. Our babies grow up to have minds of their own and often begin to make choices and take actions that we know aren't good for them.

What's comforting, however, is that everyone, even saints, have to deal with the difficulties that come as a result of being part of a family. Granted, some seemed to have had it harder than others, but few if any saints—except perhaps those who lived their entire lives in cloisters or as hermits—have escaped the stress and pain that come from being part of a family.

St. Jane de Chantal had more than her share. It began when her beloved husband, the Baron Christopher de Rabutin-Chantal, died from an accidental gunshot wound, leaving her a widow with three young children. Jane was inconsolable and despondent, falling into a deep grief-fueled depression for at least four months. For various reasons, including the protection of her children's estate, Jane was forced to live with her father-in-law, a difficult and tyrannical man who made her life miserable. For seven long years, she lived in virtual servitude, until finally, as her biographers say, her patience and virtue triumphed.

After meeting Francis de Sales, who was the bishop of Geneva, and taking him as her confessor, her difficulties eased, although she subsequently experienced struggles with her children, especially her son, Celse-Bénigne. Finally, in her later years as the foundress of numerous convents, she underwent pangs of anguish, doubt, and deep aridity. Of her and her suffering, St. Vincent de Paul said:

> She was full of faith, yet all her life had been tormented by thoughts against it. While apparently enjoying the peace and easiness of mind of souls who have reached a high state of virtue, she suffered such interior trials that she often told me her mind was so filled with all sorts of temptations and abominations that she had to strive not to look within herself. . . . But for all that suffering her face never lost its serenity, nor did she once relax in the fidelity God asked of her. And so I regard her as one of the holiest souls I have ever met on this earth.[1]

St. Vincent's words bring us to the first lesson that we can learn from St. Jane—and one that other saints have also showed us—and that is to "keep on keeping on," to use modern parlance. No matter what was going on in her life, St. Jane continued to do the next right thing—as a daughter-in-law, a parent, or a foundress.

It sounds easy enough, but it's not. When we are in pain, particularly the emotional pain that accompanies struggle and strife within a family, we are often paralyzed by indecision and handicapped by fear. We don't know what we should do, and so we do nothing except fret and fear.

The Value of Spiritual Counsel

That's where a good advisor or counselor is invaluable. St. Jane had the benefit of one of the greatest of all spiritual advisors, St. Francis de Sales. His practical advice helped Jane understand what she should be doing and, more important, when she should be doing it. For instance, she decided that God was calling her to become a nun, even though she still had young children. St. Francis advised her not to leave her children but to wait until they were old enough to be without her maternal guidance. Although entering religious life was one of the right steps for Jane, at the time she had the idea it wasn't the *next* right step, and St. Francis helped her see that.

When our lives are wounded by family members, it is imperative that we find someone who can help us gain perspective. That might be a counselor, a spiritual advisor, or just a good friend. I know that I would never have survived some of the situations I've landed in without the wit and wisdom of some close friends. They've never hesitated to tell me when I'm heading for the deep end without a life preserver, but they've also never been afraid to tell me to just put my feet down when I'm actually thrashing about in shallow waters.

But what can we learn specifically about family problems from St. Jane de Chantal?

As was said before, one of St. Jane's most difficult trials came because she truly did have a despotic father-in-law. He threatened to cut off her children's inheritance unless she came to live with him and the woman who is sometimes called his housekeeper, at other times his mistress. Whatever her role, she was just as cruel to Jane as was her father-in-law. Given her estate, Jane clearly had little recourse other than to "kill them with kindness." She unfailingly returned kindness for cruelty and patience for mistreatment. If we are in her position, having to live with in-laws or relatives who take out their anger on us, we need to try to follow her example. Now, not being saints, we may not be quite as good at it as Jane was, but we can try. We aren't necessarily called to fall in love with these difficult people, but we can treat them with civility.

Charity toward Difficult Relatives

Jane's father-in-law apparently had a change of heart toward her at the end of his life, but we can't count on that happening for us. However, being charitable toward those in the family who dislike us isn't for them; it's for us. The more we exercise self-restraint, the less likely we are to feel sorry for ourselves. Remember, self-pity only exacerbates all suffering because it makes us focus too much on ourselves and our emotions. If we can change the way we think about a situation, we can change the way we feel about it. Once our feelings are no longer trapped in a cycle of misery, we actually do feel better and suffer less. So when we don't let family members know that they are getting under our skin, they actually don't get under our skin as much. In so far as we are able, going about our business and treating our difficult in-laws with as much kindness as we can muster is sometimes not just the wisest course for reducing pain and suffering, but the only one.

However, the suffering that comes from dealing with relatives is never as painful as the suffering associated with our own children. The most excruciating pain any parent can know is to have his or her child get into trouble, particularly when that trouble carries the potential of self-destruction or even death. When a child becomes a drug addict, chooses a lifestyle that is contrary to moral teaching, or makes choices that a parent from the vantage point of age and wisdom knows are going to end up badly, what mother or father doesn't feel as if their heart is being ripped out while it's still beating?

St. Jane could identify. Her only son, Celse-Bénigne, was hot-headed, impetuous, and seemingly a bit contrary. He was also inordinately fond of dueling, an activity that could—and did—often result in serious injury and even death. The thought of that possibility agonized Jane and she prayed continually for his protection. While Celse-Bénigne did escape death by duel, he was killed on the battlefield during the campaign against the Isle of Rhé in 1627. Although married at the time, his wife died soon afterward, leaving Jane with one granddaughter, Marie de Rabutin-Chantal, the Marquise de Sévigné, who was later known for her witty and eloquent letters. (Jane did not raise Marie, who went to live with her maternal grandparents instead.)

LEARNING TO LET GO

The lesson that can be learned from Jane's relationship with her son may not be what you might expect. Yes, she prayed constantly for his well-being, and we, too, should pray for our children. But she also knew that once her child was old enough, she was no longer responsible for his actions and life decisions, and when our children reach adulthood, neither are we. Once we have fulfilled our obligations toward our children, we have to let them go. Letting go is painful, but trying to hang on too long creates additional unnecessary suffering—for them and for us. Our children can't become mature adults if we won't let go of their hands. And when we can't let go, we can't move with grace and wholeness into the next phase of our lives either.

One of the most famous stories from Jane's life illustrates this point. Apparently, Celse-Bénigne, being the only boy of the family, was a bit spoiled (even saints aren't immune from the hazards of raising entitled children!). When he was fourteen, Jane left him in the care of her father and brother, the Archbishop of Bourges, to continue his education while she took her daughters with her to found a new order of nuns, the Congregation of the Visitation. Celse-Bénigne did not like the new arrangement, so he threw himself on the threshold of the door, barring his mother's departure. "Can the tears of a child shake her resolution?" asked his tutor. "Oh, no," replied the future saint, "but after all, I am a mother!" And she stepped over the child's body to fulfill the next right thing in her life—founding a religious order.

Although fourteen may seem very young to us, Jane had made all the proper arrangements for his care, and in those times, her son was considered nearly grown up (many girls married at thirteen and boys at sixteen). Jane knew that it was time for her to be about her life and that it was time for her son to get on with his. She wasn't even removing herself completely from contact with him—the arrangement was much more like sending him off to college while she got a new job. She knew that she had given her son her love as a foundation; now he had to build on it. She had given him his roots, and now she was giving him his wings. Knowing when to let children try out their wings is one of the constant challenges of parenting. But clinging too tightly to our children creates its own kind of suffering. We need to find the balance between loving care and loving release, as St. Jane did.

Leo Tolstoy opened his famous novel *Anna Karenina* with this sentence: "Happy families are all alike; every unhappy family is unhappy in its own way." One of the reasons is that the suffering that leaves its residue of unhappiness on a family is as unique as each family member. Unlike the pain of, say, addiction, which is similar regardless of the external situation, the suffering that comes from family matters is deeply personal, and so too is the way we learn to deal with it. Perhaps St. Jane de Chantal offers us the best advice:

Fidelity toward God consists in being perfectly resigned to his holy will, in enduring everything that his goodness allows in our lives, and in carrying out all our duties, especially that of prayer, with love and for love. In prayer we must converse very familiarly with our Lord, concerning our little needs, telling him what they are, and remaining submissive to anything he may wish to do with us. . . . We should go to prayer with deep humility and an awareness of our nothingness. We must invoke the help of the Holy Spirit and that of our good angel, and then remain still in God's presence, full of faith that he is more in us than we are in ourselves. There is no danger if our prayer is without words or reflection because the good success of prayer depends neither on words nor on study. It depends upon the simple raising of our minds to God, and the more simple and stripped of feeling it is, the surer it is. We must never dwell on our sins during prayer. Regarding our offenses, a simple humbling of our soul before God, without a thought of this offense or that, is enough.[2]

FOR CONSIDERATION

1. Am I willing to look at how I might be contributing to the pain and suffering in my family life, either intentionally or unintentionally?

2. How do I treat my in-laws—as beloved parents or as troublesome nuisances? How can I grow in love for them?

3. What is my reaction when my family or my spouse's family does something that displeases me? If it is my spouse's family, do I take it out on my spouse?

4. What lessons might I be resisting that God is offering me through the struggles of family life?

5. If I have children who are approaching adulthood, have I been able to let go and let them "fly"? If I am struggling in this area, what might I do to grow in trust for the Lord's plan for their lives?

6. Do I interfere in my adult children's lives? Do I offer advice or issue orders? How can I relate to them in a way that upholds their dignity as adults?

7. Am I flexible in family matters, able to let go of the "small stuff"—things that I want my way—in order to accomplish the larger task of family harmony? How might daily prayer help me in this regard?

8. How much respect does my family have for differing ideas and opinions?

9. What might God have in mind for me after my children are grown? Am I refusing to let go of them and thereby blocking God's blessing in my own life?

Prayer

TO ST. JANE DE CHANTAL

St. Jane, renew us in the love of Jesus whose charity con-
sumed you first and foremost. In the ardor of his love, you
traversed the most various paths of life, including strife with
family members, loss of loved ones, and pain over children.
May we learn from you that love is real only when, with or
without austerities, it lives by faith, generosity, and self-renun-
ciation, in humility, simplicity, and gentleness. May we, along
with you, trust that God is with us and those we love in all
the circumstances of our lives. Amen.

— CHAPTER 10 —

Weighty Concerns

ST. FRANCIS BORGIA

Weight is a big deal—pun intended! We spend millions each year on weight-loss products and plans, all the while getting heavier and heavier. In America, 34 percent of adults are overweight, and an additional 34 percent are obese or extremely obese, according to 2007–2008 data from the Centers for Disease Control and Prevention.[1] Yet we have an almost godlike worship of celebrities who are rail thin, creating a subculture of young people—mostly girls—who literally starve themselves to look like their skeletal role models. With this sort of warped view of the body, it isn't really surprising that when a small group of young couples were questioned, three-quarters of them said they would abort a child if they knew he or she had a 50 percent chance of growing up to be obese.[2] Our mixed feelings about weight create much pain and suffering, both for those who are overweight and those who think they are.

In the first chapter, I said that most of the time suffering comes from our own choices or is something that God has allowed in order to help us learn an important lesson. The suffering that surrounds weight is, in my opinion, mostly self-created, but not in the way you might think. I say this as someone who has wrestled with weight issues most of her adult life. It's true that genetics plays some role (I come from a long line of short, fat peasants—Irish, Russian, German, take your pick), and in that sense, my body shape is something that God has allowed because of my ancestry. But while my actual weight is a result of my eating and exercise choices, that's not what I mean when I say that the suffering from being overweight is a result of my own choices.

The fact is, my weight, in and of itself, is actually neutral. God hasn't rigged a divine scale somewhere in order to make us miserable and teach us how to diet when we weigh more than some arbitrary figure on a height/weight chart. Consider that in some times and cultures, I'd be the ideal weight; perhaps I'd even be thought of as being a bit thin. I wouldn't suffer at all being the weight that I am, and I certainly wouldn't think that God was trying to punish me or teach me some lesson. However, in the culture in which I live, I see myself as being overweight and therefore judge myself. By judging myself, I create suffering that stems from my decision to judge myself. It's actually a vicious cycle, with the result being that I experience pain whenever I see a certain number on the scale, regardless of how I was feeling just moments before. It is in this sense that I am responsible for creating my own suffering when it comes to my weight.

(Now, before we go on, I realize that being overweight can result in health issues such as diabetes and heart conditions that create very real suffering and pain. However, for the purposes of this book, I consider those as part of physical suffering, not suffering from weight per se.)

When it comes to the saints, we don't really have a lot of information about their weight, probably for several reasons. First, in past centuries, only wealthy people could afford to eat enough to become overweight, and most saints weren't wealthy. Second, most saints put a good deal of emphasis on self-discipline, and one of the simplest self-disciplines is to curtail eating. Third, hagiographers don't usually give us many physical descriptions of the saints. With only portraits to go by (often painted years after the person's death), we just don't know if most saints were thin, average, or overweight. (Holy cards are not to be considered reliable images of saints.)

There are exceptions. Even in portraits, St. Thomas Aquinas is fairly substantial. And considering the nickname given to him by his classmates, "the Dumb Ox," he probably was a pretty big guy. We do know, however, beyond any doubt, that one saint was downright obese.

St. Francis Borgia (October 28, 1510–September 30, 1572), the "white" sheep of the Borgia clan (one relative was the despicable Pope Alexander VI; another, the notorious Lucrezia Borgia), was so hefty that a semicircle had to be sawed out of his table in order for him to be able to reach his food. Although we don't have any record of the suffering his weight caused him, it seems that if you are so fat that you can't sit at the table with your family without cutting a hole in it, you are going to experience some pain, both emotional and physical, from your condition.

Coming to Grips with Emotions

We don't have any of his words about how he felt about his weight, but we can still learn some lessons about weighty concerns from St. Francis. The first, and maybe the most relevant to us, is that becoming grossly overweight almost always has an emotional component attached to it. If and when we are able to come to grips with the emotions underlying our excessive eating, we stand a chance of actually making changes in our weight.

St. Francis was said to have been a pious child who wanted to become a monk (but then, most medieval saints are said to have been pious children who wanted to be monks, priests, or nuns, so this may or may not be historically accurate). His family married him off at the age of sixteen to a Portuguese noblewoman, Eleanor de Castro Melo e Menezes, with whom he had eight children. He and Eleanor seem to have had a happy marriage, and Francis appears to have been a dedicated and devout father. However, when their youngest was only seven, Eleanor died, and his biographers say that he decided he was being called to enter the newly formed Jesuit order. (He did eventually become a Jesuit and, in fact, became the third superior general of the order.)

Here's where we have to engage in a bit of speculation and reading between the lines of his dedicated hagiographers. I suspect that Francis was always on the chubby side; after all, he was a duke and had access to the very best food and wine that Italy could offer. However, since we know that he was obese prior to his becoming a Jesuit, it seems that he may have been using food as a comfort after his wife died. Overeating is certainly a common reaction to loss, and saints, while saintly, are still human. If Francis was both grieving his wife and feeling torn between wanting to join the Jesuits and being available to his children, it's no wonder that he may have packed on the pounds. We don't know for sure, but it's a plausible scenario.

He undoubtedly was under a certain amount of stress during this period of his life. Unlike a lot of medieval saints who decided to pursue the "holier" calling of priesthood after marriage,

Francis didn't immediately leave his children and head to the seminary—which would have been an acceptable and even honorable course of action. Instead, he took the road less traveled, raising his sons and daughters as a single dad until his eldest son was twenty and his youngest eleven. Now, this may seem very young to us, but remember that Francis himself was married by sixteen and a father by twenty. So by the standards of his day, Francis actually waited quite a long time, putting aside his own desires to become a priest until his children were "grown" and old enough to make their way in the world (not to mention that he left them well provided for with his estates). And even as a priest and later as a cardinal, Francis remained intimately involved with his children and grandchildren.

What does this have to do with his weight? Once he resolved the issues related to grieving his wife, raising his family, and entering religious life, he was finally able to address his weight, and eventually, "he, who was before very fat, became so lean that his servant found his clothes grown about half a yard too big for him within the space of a year."[3] When we address our emotional concerns, we, too, are often better able to deal with our weight and the issues surrounding it. As we realize more fully what God's will is for our lives, we can find the strength and courage to let go of some of the behaviors that no longer serve us or even lead us away from our life's purpose—including overeating.

Unfortunately, like many a saint, Francis was inclined to go overboard once he began to discipline his desires:

> His austerities were excessive. He entirely laid aside suppers that he might employ that time in prayer. Having passed two

Lents without taking any other sustenance than once a day a mess of leeks, or some pulse [a sort of puree of lentils or chickpeas] with a piece of bread, and a cup of water to drink, he was desirous to fast in that manner a whole year.[4]

While we might well emulate him in getting our emotional lives in order so as to best address our eating issues, we aren't obliged to copy him exactly in his dietary austerities!

BE CONSIDERATE OF OTHERS

A second lesson we can take from Francis's life is to be considerate of others and not create suffering for them because of our own personal decisions regarding food. How many times have you encountered someone who abhors red meat or who decides that only raw foods are worth eating or who has had any number of other food epiphanies and concludes that everyone should eat exactly the same way? Very often their zeal for their new diet becomes a real pain for everyone around them. Ask the person who is cooking a traditional Thanksgiving dinner and has to feed a newly converted vegan! In this we can turn to St. Francis for guidance:

At the same time he kept a table suitable to his rank for the lords who visited him, and the officers who attended him; dining with his company, he ate his leeks or pulse very slowly, and conversed facetiously with them that no one might observe him, if possible, though at table his discourse generally turned on piety.[5]

We have every right to eat the way we want; we do not have the right to subject everyone else to our choices and thereby create hardship and suffering for them. Francis was very restrained in his diet, but he didn't expect everyone who ate with him to follow suit.

FREEDOM FROM THE OPINION OF OTHERS

Another lesson we can learn from Francis is not to let the ideas of others weasel their way into our minds and cause us pain. To that end, he wrote, "We must make our way toward eternity, never regarding what men think of us or our actions, studying only to please God."[6]

Much of the suffering I've experienced about my weight is the result of my belief that others—often strangers—are constantly judging me, and that their opinions are somehow integral to my life. When I was a young mom and maybe twenty pounds over my optimal weight, a young child came up to me on the playground and, prompted by his mother who stood encouragingly in the background, said to me, "You're FAT! Why don't you go on a diet?" He then ran proudly back to his mother, who smiled at him and smirked at me. His comment and her smirk smarted for years until I finally realized that I was letting strangers live rent free in my mind and influence how I felt about myself. It was only after I decided not to take to heart what others think that I was able to have pity for someone who would send a child to insult a stranger.

The fact is, I don't believe the suffering we experience from weight comes from God, but it can be returned to God. When we ask ourselves what God would want us to do, not what the culture or other people expect of us, we are much more likely to be freed from the pain of weighty issues and, at the same time, find a way to resolve them—which may mean losing weight or may mean learning self-acceptance. In either case, the pain and suffering associated with weight will be reduced or removed, and we can begin to live more in grace than in groveling. When I concluded that my weight wasn't a matter for public discussion but something between God and me, I found much more peace about the numbers on the scale, and I suspect that any of you who struggle with weighty matters will as well.

Before we leave the subject of weight and suffering, I'd like to touch briefly on the opposite problem—being too thin. Because our culture believes that "you can never be too rich or too thin," those who suffer from anorexia are not viewed with the same disdain as those who are obese. But anyone who has experienced an eating disorder or who has loved someone who has such a disorder knows that anorexia carries its own pain and dangers, not the least of which is the very real possibility of premature death. The lessons we can draw from St. Francis Borgia are equally applicable to both sides of weighty suffering.

When it comes to how we should treat our bodies, perhaps the best example is the saint for whom Francis Borgia himself was named. St. Francis of Assisi admitted near the end of his life that he had been a bit too harsh toward himself and asked forgiveness from "Brother Ass," his term for his body. May we, too, learn not to be too hard toward our bodies lest we create suffering that God does not intend for us.

FOR CONSIDERATION

1. What do I think is God's opinion about my weight? Does he judge me for how much I weigh? Do I think I can please him if I am more disciplined about what I eat? Do I think he will love me more if I am at my optimal weight?

2. How do I view my body? Is it my "enemy" or my "friend"? Do I see it as a gift from God, to be treated with reverence and care?

3. Do I obsess about food? If so, how can I view diet in a more positive, life-giving way?

4. Do I pay too much attention to what others think I should weigh? What might help me to focus less on others' opinions?

5. What emotional issues might I be trying to avoid by overeating or eating too little?

6. Do I make those around me suffer because of my issues with food? If so, what might I do to change? Can I be more flexible?

7. How does it change my mind about sanctity to know that saints like Francis Borgia and Catherine of Siena (who ate very little) had issues with weight and food?

8. Do I equate thinness with goodness? Do I look to thin celebrities as my role models for a fulfilled life?

9. What steps can I take right now to eliminate the pain I have created in my life around food and weight?

Prayer

OF ST. FRANCIS BORGIA

My Lord and my refuge!
What did you find in me so that you took me into account?
What did you see in me so that you wanted me in
your Company?

I feel myself to be a coward, dependent upon the world
that surrounds me, full of self-love.
Lord, what did you find in me?

With good reason the angels praise you with awe.
And I, too, praise you after being disconcerted,
discovering how, from such weak foundations,
you wish to raise up your works.

How to respond, O Lord, to your tenderness?
How to respond to your love?

I do not possess the capacity to understand
nor the words to express—indeed, I hear and I see
that not only do you pardon my faults,
but you also invite me and call me to your Company.[7]

— CHAPTER 11 —

Prejudice

VENERABLE PIERRE TOUSSAINT AND

ST. JOSEPHINE BAKHITA

Wthen we think about prejudice, we often think about attitudes involving the color of one's skin. But people from all over the world suffer from prejudice, and skin color is not the only basis for prejudice and discrimination. For example, the Tutsis and Hutus in Rwanda had the same color skin, but their tribal rivalries resulted in mass genocide. In our own country at the turn of the last century, the Irish, a fair-skinned people if ever there was one, often were victims of discrimination. In many parts of the world today, women are discriminated against. For discrimination to happen, all it takes is for one group to have power and decide that another group is not as valuable, as worthy, or even as human.

So what can we learn about how to deal with suffering from prejudice and discrimination? Because prejudice is the result of sin, whether individual or collective, we might think that the only lesson it might bear for us is to eliminate any of our own prejudices. Of course, that is a lesson, and a valuable one, but when we look at the life of Venerable Pierre Toussaint (1766– June 30, 1853), we discover that there are, indeed, some deeper lessons to explore.

117

Pierre Toussaint was born into slavery in Haiti. To escape the Haitian revolution of 1787, he, his sister Rosalie, and a few other slaves were sent by their master to accompany their mistress to New York. When his master died, leaving his wife penniless, Pierre, who had been trained as a hairdresser, began to support her. Even though he became a wealthy man and bought his sister's freedom, he remained a slave himself until his mistress's death, believing that it would be easier for her to accept his help as her servant rather than as an equal. She freed him on her deathbed, and he and his wife went on to become some of New York's great philanthropists, using their home as a shelter for orphans, a refuge for the destitute, a home for priests, and the headquarters for a credit bureau and an employment agency. He was also a major contributor to the building of St. Patrick's Cathedral, although as a black man he was not allowed to enter the church.

His funeral Mass packed St. Peter's, the church where it was held. Bear in mind that slavery was still legal at the time, so the words of one of New York's elite, Philip Schuyler, a descendant of Alexander Hamilton, demonstrate just how remarkable Pierre must have been: "I have known Christians who were not gentlemen, and gentlemen who were not Christians, but one man I know who was both—and that man was black."[1]

His praise leads me to the first lesson we can draw from Venerable Pierre's life: Even when we experience suffering from prejudice, we must not return evil for evil or pain for pain. Clearly, Pierre suffered. Not being allowed to enter the cathedral he had helped to build, being treated as a domestic servant when he was actually supporting his mistress and her lifestyle, and never being permitted on the public omnibuses only because he was black must have been extremely painful. Regardless of what he was feeling, however, Pierre never was known to react with bitterness or anger but was unfailingly kind and generous.

It's a tough lesson for most of us because our natural reaction to mistreatment is to strike back. However, becoming involved in an escalating battle of retaliation always creates more pain for us. It's inevitable; we cannot attempt to inflict pain on another without having that pain circle back to us. The sad reality is that sometimes, as Pierre's life shows us, we don't have a choice between suffering and no suffering but between suffering and more suffering. Making the decision to try our best to respond to others with civility and respect will always have a positive effect, both on us and on those to whom we are directing our response.

Which brings us to a second lesson we might learn from Pierre: By projecting love to all, even in the face of prejudice for his skin color, Pierre had a remarkable and life-altering influence on everyone he met, black and white alike:

> Many of New York's "first families" vied with each other in claiming the dignified, gentle black man as their counselor, one in whom they could safely confide and whose advice they gladly followed. Many called him "Our St. Pierre." This relationship was unprecedented in post-Revolutionary America, when racial and religious prejudices ran high.[2]

We, too, have an effect on those we meet, for good or for bad. Recently someone contacted me via Facebook who had been the front-desk manager at a hotel where I had often stayed when I was traveling for my job. I'm hardly a saint—but she said that my attitude had been partially responsible for her return to the Catholic Church! To say that I was shocked is an understatement. I honestly don't remember ever talking to her about faith or religion or church, but apparently (*Deo gratias!*) something about the way I behaved made an impression on her. I don't know what that might have been, but the one thing I do know is that I try to live by the Golden Rule of treating others as I would like to be treated. In this case, I must have done better than I had imagined. Her words were a vivid reminder to me that we can carry the spark of the divine into our ordinary lives, something Pierre did with aplomb. In fact, one of his admirers at the time of his death called him "God's reflection in ebony."

CHOOSING HAPPINESS

A final lesson we can draw from the life of Pierre and his response to prejudice is that no matter what situation we may find ourselves in, we can have a "good life." This is not to deny the impact of unfair, oppressive, or sad events; we all experience them to some degree or another, and those who are victims of prejudice often experience them in the extreme. But as Abraham Lincoln said, "Most folks are as happy as they make up their minds to be." It seems as if Pierre made up his mind to be happy regardless of his state in life. He loved his wife, Juliette Noel: "I would not change her for all the ladies in the world! She is beautiful in my eyes." Pierre and Juliette doted on their adopted daughter, Euphemia, and Pierre appears to have taken pride in his ability as a hairdresser. From him we can learn that living in a state of gratitude for what we have, not constantly dwelling on what is out of our reach, is a key component for a fulfilled life. It doesn't mean that a so-called attitude of gratitude will eliminate all suffering, especially the suffering that comes from something so outside our control as prejudice, but it does mean that unnecessary, self-imposed suffering can be reduced or even eliminated. We can find happiness and goodness in our lives because, as it is often said, "Happiness is an inside job!" If given the choice between misery and happiness, even in the midst of pain, we can choose happiness. It may not eliminate the suffering, but then again, it just might.

Before we leave this chapter, I want to point out that even when saints are placed in similar situations, they don't always have similar reactions to their suffering. We are each individuals on our own individual journey to wholeness and holiness, and therefore there is no such thing as a single path that is "saintly." For instance, one of the hallmarks of Pierre's life was that he remained a slave even when he had the means to purchase his freedom. St. Josephine Bakhita (ca. 1869–February 8, 1947), on the other hand, made a very different choice. Born in Sudan, she was sold at least five times to different masters, finally ending up as the slave of an Italian diplomat. During her years in slavery, she was cruelly treated and even tortured with beatings and whippings that resulted in scarring. Through a variety of circumstances, she ended up living in the convent of the Canossian Sisters in Venice. When her mistress wanted her to return to servitude, Josephine refused. Her case ended up in the Italian courts, which declared that since Italian law didn't permit slavery, Josephine was free. She elected to join the sisters permanently, becoming Sr. Josephine Margarita Afortunada (her original name, *Bakhita*, is Arabic for "lucky.").

Both Pierre and Josephine were slaves and both suffered from prejudice because of their skin color, but they had very different reactions to remaining in slavery. Pierre worked within his situation; Josephine escaped it. One choice wasn't "right" and the other "wrong." They were simply the choices those individuals made that were the best for them at the time. For Pierre, remaining a slave, albeit a humanely treated one, was how he could best bear witness to his faith. For Josephine, returning to slavery would have meant giving up her religious vocation, and her vocation was something she felt God was asking of her. Both followed what they believed to be God's direction for their lives.

When we are coping with suffering—not just from prejudice but suffering of any kind—we can look to these two holy people and realize that we have options available for how we choose to react to it. We can elect to remain in the situation, using it for our own development and the growth of others, or we can do whatever we can to free ourselves in order to fulfill our purpose in life. It is only through prayerful consideration that we can know which choice is right for us.

Prejudice as well as its concomitant suffering remains one of the great ills of the world. In addition to learning lessons from the lives of Venerable Pierre and St. Josephine, we must also do our part to eliminate this scourge. We can do it one person, one action, one prayer at a time.

FOR CONSIDERATION:

1. Am I guilty of prejudices against people of a different race, ethnic background, religion, or culture? Am I willing to let go of any prejudices and instead recognize our common humanity?

2. Have I ever been the object of prejudice? Has my family? If so, how did I deal with the situation? Did I feel free to respond in a way that differed from other people who were also being discriminated against?

3. Do I live by the Golden Rule in my life, even with people I don't know or like?

4. Do I allow the circumstances of my life to dictate how I feel? How would an "attitude of gratitude" help me?

5. How do I respond when someone treats me badly? Do I lash out in return? What might help me to avoid such a reaction so that I can respond in kindness?

6. How happy do I allow myself to be? Do I believe that my happiness is really in my control? How does my relationship with God help me to be happy?

7. Do I stand up for my rights when I believe it is in my best interest to do so? In what way might my circumstances of life allow me to be an effective witness to the power of love?

8. How might I reach out to people who are different from me, including those in my parish or neighborhood?

Prayer
TO PIERRE TOUSSAINT

Pierre Toussaint, you practiced an extraordinary compassion and charity and shared your kindness, wisdom, prayers, time, and means with countless persons. I sometimes find it difficult to be charitable, especially with (name) or in these circumstances (describe circumstances).

Obtain for me from God the virtue of charity. Then I may rejoice one day with God and all his saints in heaven.

This I ask in Jesus' name. Amen.[3]

PIERRE TOUSSAINT'S DEATHBED PRAYER

God is with me,
I want nothing on the earth.[4]

— CHAPTER 12 —

Temptation to Vice

STS. FRANCIS, CAMILLUS, ROMUALD,

AND OTHERS

Using the words "vice" and "saint" in the same sentence may seem a bit disrespectful. The very idea of a saint struggling with immoral, illegal, or inappropriate behavior doesn't seem to fit in with our ideas about saints and who they are. After all, saints are, well, saintly, and vice is not.

What we are talking about here, however, is temptation and the suffering associated with it, not the vice itself. The internal battle to stop ourselves from acting on a desire is not the same as dealing with the consequences of having acted upon that desire. And to be sure, saints suffered from temptations even if they didn't succumb to them—and even after they were recognized for their holiness.

This is where the desire of admirers to make sure that saints always look good can sometimes serve to our detriment. Biographers are willing to acknowledge that some saints had colorful pasts, but because many hagiographers wanted to ensure that their favorite saints got all the recognition for holiness that they deserved, they sometimes glossed over certain very human tendencies. Later readers can end up with the idea that once a saint embarked on the path to holiness, all of that person's former temptations were left behind, never to be revisited. That leads us to believe that the heroes of the faith somehow had an easier time reaching sanctity than the rest of us would, which is not true. In reality, almost all the saints encountered some bumps along the way simply because they were human. It's just that we don't hear about their struggles as often as we do their miracles!

A good example is St. Francis of Assisi. While we all have heard stories about his rowdy youth, we tend to slide right over them and see him only as the wild ascetic in the wilderness renouncing everything for the love of God. He was that, true, but he was also a flesh-and-blood man until the end of his life. In fact, so the story goes, when he was proclaimed to be a living saint by one of his admirers, he gave a surprising answer (surprising to them and surprising to us): "Do not declare me a saint yet. I am still perfectly capable of fathering children." The very idea that St. Francis would even have such a thought will probably shock more than a few readers. Yet when praised for his sanctity, he apparently remained well aware enough of his sexual nature to make that his first response. (He also loved marzipan cookies and asked for them on his deathbed, so he didn't lose all his love of life's pleasures, despite his austerities.)

This is not to imply that Francis had an unusual struggle with any particular vice, sexual or not. But certainly other saints have experienced ongoing suffering because of the tug toward temptations of various sorts.

St. Camillus de Lellis (May 25, 1550–July 14, 1614) loved gambling, and this is one of the first things mentioned in any biography of him. For his biographers to give it such a prominent place gives us a pretty good hint that it must have been a major struggle for him. St. Benedict (ca. 480–547), the founder of Western monasticism, was well-known for having a violent temper. Even the unexpected sight of a woman caused St. Bernard of Clairvaux (1090–August 20, 1153) to jump into an icy stream to quell his desires. (Talk about a cold shower!) St. Romuald (ca. 950–1027) a restorer of the Order of St. Benedict, suffered so much from what he called "temptations of the flesh" that he often took off to hunt alone in the woods until he had regained his self-control. Blessed Pier Giorgio Frassati (April 6, 1901–July 4, 1925) was a smoker (as were many other saints). And, of course, St. Augustine (354–430) discusses the struggle he had with chastity in his famous *Confessions*.

Temptation to vice isn't limited to males, of course. I'm sure some women saints suffered from temptations over the centuries, but other than the ever popular "repentant prostitute" such as St. Mary of Egypt, their struggles are largely hidden from history. Apparently, if it is unseemly for a male saint to face vice, it is even more so for a female. One woman who might have had a tendency toward a mild vice is Brigit of Ireland, who was very fond of beer. A famous Celtic poem attributed to her contains these lines: "I should like a great lake of ale / for the King of the Kings. / I should like the family of heaven / to be drinking it through time eternal."

The guidance we can glean from the example of the saints when it comes to the pain created by vice and its temptations isn't quite the same as that of other suffering. One reason is that the way the saints dealt with these issues (especially those saints from the more distant past) isn't always applicable for us today. Stripping off all your clothes and rolling in a briar patch, as St.

Francis did, or leaping into the nearest river, like St. Bernard, is probably going to get you taken in for a psychiatric evaluation, not win you respect as a sign of your holiness.

Moreover, temptation by its very nature is individual, so what works to resist vice for one person might not work for another. Trying to use the unique methods of a specific saint for dealing with his particular temptation sometimes isn't all that helpful. To give a personal example, I have a weakness for potato chips. A well-meaning friend told me that baked kale leaves sprinkled with sea salt are "just as good" as potato chips and will quench any craving for a salty snack. I'm glad it works for her, but let's just say that baked kale and dip isn't going to be my "go-to" snack for banishing the desire for chips any time soon!

We All Experience Temptation

Given those caveats, the lessons I've learned from the saints about temptation are fourfold. The foundational lesson is that temptation is universal; everyone has to deal with it—even saints. Once we accept the reality that we are going to experience temptation, we can be better prepared to cope with it. To be forewarned is to be forearmed.

So how did the saints in general deal with their temptations?

Distraction is a major technique. Now, a lot of them took distraction to an extreme (briar patches and icy streams, for example), but their basic premise was sound. When faced with temptation, find something that will divert your attention and keep your mind engrossed in it. When I'm sorely tempted to finish the last of the pan of brownies and have spent too much time wrestling to resist the urge, I go clean the kitty litter; my desire for anything chocolate immediately subsides. Of course, you don't have to choose a distraction that repulses you. St. Romuald enjoyed hunting, so mounting his horse and heading into the woods in order to divert himself from his fleshly temptations wasn't necessarily self-punishment. A major reason why we suffer from our temptations is because we dwell on them. Breaking the cycle with a distraction—especially with something we enjoy—will almost always remove the suffering (at least temporarily).

Another method employed by most saints is old-fashioned avoidance, what used to be called avoiding "the near occasion of sin." If something tempts you, either remove it or remove yourself. This is the method that Camillus de Lellis apparently used with gambling. While he was in the military, he gambled excessively. It was only after he left the army for good and entered the nursing profession (where the temptation to gamble was greatly reduced) that he was able to conquer his tendencies.

Dieters use this technique all the time by removing any foods from their sight or reach that are off-limits, but it can be extended to any temptation. If you know it's going to affect you, don't allow it into your life. Of course, that's easier said than done, but a final lesson from the saints can make it easier.

Asking for God's Help

St. Alfonsus Liguori, who experienced his own lifelong suffering, explains this final lesson on how saints—and the rest of us—can cope with the suffering that comes from temptations:

Without prayer, it is impossible to resist temptations and to keep the commandments. Moreover, prayer is the most necessary weapon of defense against our enemies; he who does not avail himself of it, says St. Thomas [Aquinas], is lost. He does not doubt that Adam fell because he did not recommend himself to God when he was tempted: "He sinned because he had not recourse to the divine assistance." . . .

St. Bernard's teaching is the same: "What are we, or what is our strength, that we should be able to resist so many temptations? This certainly it was that God intended; that we, seeing our deficiencies, and that we have no other help, should with all humility have recourse to his mercy."[1]

What we cannot do on our own, we can with the assistance of God. How many times do we experience pain and suffering from our temptations and vices when the way out lies directly in front of us, and we simply haven't asked for it? In some ways, it reminds me of a "hidden object" video game. If you aren't familiar with the genre, such games challenge the player to sort through a scene to find something hidden in the image. I can look for the longest time without seeing whatever it is I'm searching for, and then when I finally use the hint button, it suddenly becomes so obvious. How could I have overlooked it for so long? The same is true when it comes to the pain of temptation and not asking God for help. When we finally do ask for help, we are often surprised that the aid comes so quickly and effectively. We really shouldn't be surprised, since almost two thousand years ago, St. Paul, an authority on both suffering and temptation, said:

No testing has overtaken you that is not common to everyone. God is faithful, and he will not let you be tested beyond your strength, but with the testing he will also provide the way out so that you may be able to endure it. (1 Corinthians 10:13)

Of course, the key is to ask for the help. In fact, every time we say the Our Father, we ask, "Lead us not into temptation." Now, that doesn't mean that God is the one who tempts us. Instead, we are asking that God protect us from our own temptations. That may be the most important lesson we can take from the saints and temptation—to ask for divine assistance when we need it and to believe that it will, indeed, be given.

FOR CONSIDERATION

1. Am I aware of my temptations so that they don't throw me off guard when they come? What might help me to be forewarned and therefore forearmed?

2. What is my greatest temptation? Do I recognize it as a temptation when I am in the midst of struggling with it? Do I turn to God for assistance?

3. When I am tempted, how do I respond? Do I try to remove myself from the temptation or remove the temptation itself? How well does that work?

4. Have I found my own individual way of responding to a temptation, one that works for me?

5. What sorts of things can I use to distract myself when I'm feeling tempted? What activities do I enjoy that I could turn to so that I can take my focus off my temptation?

6. When has God delivered me from a temptation? What happened? Do I really believe that God will help me find a way out if I ask?

Prayer

THE LORICA OF GILDAS (ABRIDGED)

This prayer is called a "lorica," or a prayer of protection. The name probably comes from St. Paul. In Latin, the words from Ephesians 6:14, "put on the breastplate of righteousness," are translated as *"induti lorica iustitiae."*

> God the unconquerable guardian,
> defend me on every side by thy power.
> Free Thou all limbs of mine,
> with Thy safe shield protecting each,
> so that the fell demons brandish not
> against my sides, as is their wont, their darts. . . .
> Cover, therefore, O God, with strong corslet . . .
> Cover me all in all with my five senses, . . .
> so that, from my soles to the top of the head,

in no member, without within, may I be sick; . . .
Until, with the gift of old age from God,
I blot out my sins with good works;
And, in departing from the flesh, be free from stain,
and be able to fly to the heights,
and, by the mercy of God, be borne in joy
to the heavenly cool retreats of His kingdom.
Amen.[2]

CHAPTER 13

Financial Stress

ST. ELIZABETH ANN SETON

Because she is the first native-born American saint, many people know the life story of St. Elizabeth Ann Seton (August 28, 1774–January 4, 1821). Her conversion from devout Anglican, her struggles to live her new faith, and her impressive accomplishments (she started what would eventually become the parochial school system in America and founded the Sisters of Charity) are as much a part of U.S. history as they are of hallowed hagiography.

What many people might not realize, however, is that throughout much of her adult life, St. Elizabeth faced a suffering all too common today: severe financial stress. From the time that she and her husband went bankrupt early in their marriage, until her later years, when she struggled to maintain her convents and sisters, Elizabeth knew firsthand what it was like to suffer from lack of funds and experience involuntary poverty.

Poverty is a rather odd animal in Christian teaching. On the one hand, it is highly praised as an ideal lifestyle for a Christian believer since it allows one to emulate Jesus more closely. On the other hand, most of the saints who have espoused radical poverty were celibate members of religious communities and so didn't have to worry about feeding, clothing, and sheltering a family. Moreover, Jesus himself said that he came to bring abundant life (John 10:10), and abundance (which can be defined as an extremely plentiful or overly sufficient quantity or supply) and poverty (the state or condition of having little or no money, goods, or means of support) don't really mesh. It's hard to have more than enough when you don't have anywhere near enough. Even if Jesus were speaking only of an abundant spiritual life, as many have argued, nowhere in Scripture is poverty, in and of itself, seen as a blessing. If poverty were truly a great blessing, then heaven would be envisioned not as a place where all good things are given to us but as a place of extreme lack and destitution.

Furthermore, although Jesus was born in a cave or stable, and although he probably only had his basic needs met during his public ministry, his family was not destitute. Joseph is described in Matthew 13:55 as a *tekton*, a Greek word meaning "carpenter" or "builder"—a skilled workman more along the lines of what we would call a mason or even a contractor. He wasn't whittling the occasional little bench or stool for his neighbors in exchange for a handful of grapes. He probably was involved in much larger construction projects, possibly even working in the nearby Roman city of Caesarea, where massive public building was going on.

So it seems to me that instead of calling them "poor," it is much more realistic to think of the Holy Family as "average"— not the elite with their marbled baths and elaborate banquets, but a family with adequate food, sufficient clothing, and a satisfactory dwelling to be able to live a normal life. In other words, the Holy Family was pretty much just an ordinary family doing ordinary things. My point is not to say that Jesus was rich; he wasn't. My point is to show that suffering from severe financial hardship doesn't have to be considered a goal of our lives just because we have been taught that Jesus and the Holy Family were "poor." Jesus said he came to bring us abundant life, not neediness and poverty. Moreover, being poor and in debt doesn't automatically create holiness. If it did, the crime rates in slums and inner cities would be the lowest anywhere.

Of course, wealth brings its own set of temptations and struggles, but the reality is that even saints need money to do their good works, even if they merely have the money long enough to give it away. The only time that poverty is a true blessing is when it is voluntary. Having to worry about where the next meal comes from is suffering, not grace.

That's why Elizabeth Ann Seton's money struggles provide such real-life lessons. She had to figure out how to get enough money to build her schools and provide for her nuns. And if she were merely the founder of a religious community, it might have been one thing to be destitute, but she had five children to take care of as well.

Elizabeth was not accustomed to poverty. Her father was a well-to-do physician and she married the heir to a successful shipping business. Unfortunately, her husband, William, was not quite the businessman his father had been, and not long after their marriage, in the words of the time, "their fortune declined." Within three years they were bankrupt, and Elizabeth had to return to her father's home with their children. When William's health failed, a physician suggested a sea voyage, so Elizabeth sold all she had to finance a trip to Italy. Tragically, William died about a month after they landed there. When Elizabeth returned to New York, she had to live off the kindness of friends. Eventually, she turned to teaching as a way to support herself and her children and ended up establishing a community of sisters devoted to education.

TRUSTING IN GOD

Elizabeth's life and her ongoing struggle with the lack of money can be an inspiration to those of us who also face financial stress. One of the first lessons we can learn from her is that we, like Elizabeth, must let go of fear, trusting that God will provide. Although William was sure he was headed for debtors' prison, Elizabeth maintained a steadfast conviction that somehow it would all work out. When we are faced with mounting debt and no way to pay it off, we have two choices—either we can despair or we can trust that we will be shown a solution. Despair only increases our suffering, adding unnecessarily to our pain. Trust allows us to think more clearly and thereby see options that might not have been visible when we were blinded by fear. However, as with many things, the choice between trust and despair is always ours.

A second lesson we can learn from Elizabeth is that while trusting that God will provide is important, on a practical level, we also have to do our part. Elizabeth needed to find a way to support her family. She hadn't planned on being a teacher, but when the opportunity to teach arose, she took it. Moreover, even though she had a gift for teaching, she didn't give it away; she charged her students. She realized that she had to make money, not just expect it to appear out of thin air.

Sometimes we get the mistaken idea that it isn't "spiritual" to use our talents to make money, but even the Scriptures say that the workman is worthy of pay (1 Timothy 5:18). If we are in financial difficulty and have an ability or talent, we are duty bound to use it in order to support ourselves and our families.

Since using our talents is always the will of God, it's a sure and safe place to begin. St. Elizabeth's own words confirm this: "The first end I propose in our daily work is to do the will of God; secondly, to do it in the manner he wills it; and thirdly, to do it because it is his will."[1]

But what if you don't really know what it is that you should be doing? St. Elizabeth faced the same problem. Before she discovered her talent for teaching, she had tried several other ways to support her family, none of which worked out. But she simply kept trying various things until the right door opened. We must do the same. We simply have to keep looking for the kind of work that will both allow us to take care of our needs and utilize the gifts we have been given, no matter how long it may take. The prayer Elizabeth prayed before her conversion to Catholicism can be of aid here: "If I am right, thy grace impart still in the right to say. If I am wrong, oh, teach my heart to find the better way."[2] In other words, we ask to continue on the path if we are on the right one; if we aren't, then we ask to be shown the right direction.

ASKING FOR HELP

A third lesson from St. Elizabeth is difficult for many of us, including me: Ask for help, especially with finances. This goes against every grain in my body (and probably yours too), but think of it this way: Our asking makes it possible for others to give. St. Elizabeth was raised in upper-class New York society with its galas and balls. When her own daughters reached the age when a young woman is presented to society, she (wisely) did not automatically assume that they were going to enter religious life, so she planned for their debut. However, she had no money to provide the dresses and accoutrements necessary and was forced to ask her former society friends to contribute. For a woman who had once been part of that crowd, it must have been humbling to make such a request. Sometimes when we are in a financial bind, we, too, must accept assistance. Relying entirely on others is not the answer to our financial troubles, but if we must, we need to do so with humility and gratitude.

A final lesson from Elizabeth's life might be categorized as a cross between a warning and an encouragement. Earlier we talked about how sometimes our suffering can be self-generated. Even saints aren't immune from this. At least some of St. Elizabeth's financial woes were created because she went against her own better judgment. When the doctor suggested that a trip to Italy might help William's failing health, Elizabeth had her doubts, but she sold all their possessions anyway. Had she not done so, had they not made the voyage, her life might not have had as many financial stresses. However, "we know that all things work together for good for those who love God, who are called according to his purpose" (Romans 8:28). In Italy she became acquainted with Catholicism. Had she not made the voyage, she may never have converted, founded the Sisters of Charity, or become a saint.

Her example can be a comfort to those of us who have made inopportune financial decisions. Even in the midst of our trials and suffering, blessings can still emerge. We may have to endure the consequences and subsequent pain that result from our choices, but in Elizabeth's words, "We know certainly that our God calls us to a holy life. We know that he gives us every grace, every abundant grace; and though we are so weak of ourselves, this grace is able to carry us through every obstacle and difficulty."[3]

Even finances.

FOR CONSIDERATION

1. How much of my time and energy is taken up with financial concerns?

2. Do I truly believe that there is an answer to my financial needs? Why or why not?

3. It is said that God helps them who help themselves. What am I doing on a practical level to eliminate my problems with money?

4. How can I grow in gratitude for what I do have, no matter how much or how little?

5. How willing am I to share with others from both my basic needs as well as my surplus?

6. What do I think Jesus meant by an "abundant life"? How do I see it manifested in my life?

7. Deep down, do I believe that money is the root of all evil? (The actual Scripture verse, 1 Timothy 6:10, is this: "Love of money is a root of all kinds of evil.") Why or why not?

8. What would I do if I had no financial worries? What good might I be able to do that I can't do right now?

9. Have I asked God to show me the way out of my financial struggle? Am I listening to the answer?

Prayer

OF ST. ELIZABETH ANN SETON

O Father, the first rule of our dear Savior's life
was to do Your Will.
Let His Will of the present moment
be the first rule of our daily life and work,
with no other desire
but for its most full and complete accomplishment.
Help us to follow it faithfully,
so that doing what You wish
we will be pleasing to You. Amen.[4]

CHAPTER 14

Grief

ST. ELIZABETH OF HUNGARY

The Welsh poet Dylan Thomas wrote, "After the first death, there is no other."[1] Some have interpreted that line to be a poetic way of saying, "We only die once," but like all good poetry, it is subject to a variety of interpretations. For me, it has always meant that once you truly experience the profound suffering that comes from losing a loved one, you'll never experience grief in the same way again. That "first death" may not necessarily be the first time you experience death; rather, it's the first time you experience it in a way that wrenches your heart and soul.

As I write this, I am mourning the loss of my mother, who died at the age of ninety-two after a lengthy period of decline. While my heart aches, hers was not my "first death." I experienced that some years ago when, of all things, a beloved cat died. It was then that I was utterly struck by the soul-wrenching experience of grief and the pain that it brings. Of course, the grief from the loss of a pet, no matter how beloved, differs from the loss of a human being, as it rightly should. But the one thing that I learned from that "first death" was how I process grief and the various emotions that characterize it, from denial, anger, and bargaining to depression and acceptance.

The fact is that we all process grief in our own unique ways. You might be stoic, keeping a steely countenance and dealing with the emotions internally. Or you might be more vocal in your suffering, wailing both literally and figuratively. The comfort that comes after you have once experienced real grief is that from then on, you know your own reaction—the way you will cope and process it. And you also know that you will get through it. Along with recognizing the stages of pain, you begin to see the stages of healing as well.

I know that I tend to become ensnared by depression and deep sadness before I finally come to acceptance. After a grievous loss, even the sunniest days are tinged with gray clouds in my soul. But I also know that when I first begin to sense a quickening of hope and a feeling of calmness, no matter how momentary, the healing is beginning. It may take a long time, especially when the loss is as profound as that of a mother, but having lived through grief before, I also know that healing will come in its own time and in its own way.

SAINTS GRIEVE TOO

The saints were not immune from the suffering that comes from loss and grief. No one is; it's part of the human condition. St. Therese of Lisieux was deeply affected by the death of her mother and father. St. Jane de Chantal fell into such a deep depression after the death of her husband that her family worried for her health. St. Francis Borgia mourned his wife for much of the rest of his life. Blessed Pope John Paul II said that it was out of the loss of his mother that he developed his great love and devotion to the Blessed Mother. Of all the saints, however, it is Elizabeth of Hungary whose deep suffering from grief has lessons we all can learn from.

A thirteenth-century princess, Elizabeth was married at the age of fourteen to Ludwig IV of Thuringia. By all accounts they seem to have been soul mates. Deeply in love, they had three children and appeared destined to live "happily ever after." However, on his way to join the Crusades, Ludwig died of the Black Death on September 11, 1227. Elizabeth was only twenty. When the news reached her in October, just after she had given birth to a daughter, she is said to have cried out, "The world with all its joys is now dead to me."

For some time afterward, Elizabeth fell into a deep depression as she grieved the loss of her beloved husband. However, she eventually emerged from her suffering and grief to become honored, even after all these centuries, as one of the great saints of Europe. Her experience of walking through mourning provides those of us who also mourn a profound example.

The first lesson we can learn from her is that she fully experienced her pain. When Ludwig's body was finally returned, she buried it in the family vault and was said to have wept bitterly and almost inconsolably. She didn't try to minimize her anguish or brush it aside. She embraced it and recognized that upon Ludwig's death, for a while at least, all the joys of the world were dead to her. That state of mind is one that we who have grieved know all too well. It's difficult to experience anything joyful when body and soul are entrapped in sorrow. What we need to realize is that if we don't allow ourselves to experience our pain and suffering while grieving, it won't just "go away." Our feelings become submerged and can often resurface in the form of anger, depression, addiction, or other unhealthy ways.

We need to "feel the feelings" first so that they can eventually be transformed.

Jesus gives us the prime example of how to grieve openly. When his friend Lazarus died, Jesus wept.

> When Mary came where Jesus was and saw him, she knelt at his feet and said to him, "Lord, if you had been here, my brother would not have died." When Jesus saw her weeping, and the Jews who came with her also weeping, he was greatly disturbed in spirit and deeply moved. He said, "Where have you laid him?" They said to him, "Lord, come and see." Jesus began to weep. (John 11:32-35)

Jesus felt the pain of the loss of his friend, and he allowed himself to experience that suffering. He wept and mourned, even though he knew that "this illness does not lead to death; rather it is for God's glory, so that the Son of God may be glorified through it" (John 11:4). His example serves as our example as well: The only way out of grief is through it.

GRIEVING TAKES TIME

Grieving takes time. It isn't over and done with in the days from the death to the funeral. St. Elizabeth's life shows us that even saints need time to work through their pain. Elizabeth gave herself time to process the pain. For several months, until the following Good Friday, she withdrew into herself, allowing the passing months and God's grace to bring about healing. We can only guess that she went through the motions of court life dressed in widow's garb and caring for her children, all the while bearing in her heart her great pain. Finally, at the end of Lent, she reemerged into life.

And that provides us with another important lesson about grief: Elizabeth did not permit herself to become enchained and ensnared by continual ruminations over her loss. She drew a deep breath, figuratively speaking, and resumed her own existence.

The first thing she did was recommit her life to God. We don't know what she was thinking about during the months of mourning, but we do know that once they had passed, she sought to fulfill God's will for the rest of her life. She joined the Third Order of St. Francis, becoming one of the first to do so, and rededicated her life to works of charity. It seems quite fitting that she did this during Holy Week, using the experience of Lent to grieve the loss of her former life, and then, during Easter, embracing her new and deeply changed way of life as her own "new normal."

Which brings us to the third thing about grief that we can learn from Elizabeth: She began serving others. In the summer of 1228, she built a hospital and took on nursing duties for the sick, an activity that she pursued until her own untimely death at the age of twenty-four. Her action shows us that no matter how painful our losses, we are not to become stuck in the suffering. Rather, suffering can become a way for us to engage more fully with life. We can allow our grief to deepen our own spiritual lives, and we can help others with their suffering.

While the greatest of our suffering from grief comes from the loss of our loved ones, grieving isn't limited to death. We grieve all the "little deaths" that come with life: reversal of finances, betrayal, unemployment, theft, accidents, loss of relationships, disappointments, accidents, crime, or forced relocations. Grieving can happen anytime that something dear to us is taken away.

Since none of us will get through this life without losing something, we will all experience grief. It's what we do with that pain—what lessons we allow ourselves to learn and how that suffering can bring us to a greater understanding of ourselves and our purpose here on earth—that really matters.

FOR CONSIDERATION

1. What was the "first death" I experienced? What did I learn from that experience about the unique way I deal with grief?

2. In what ways can I be more fully present to those who are mourning? How can I reach out to them and comfort them?

3. If I am currently grieving a loss of any kind, what can I do today on a practical level to help get outside of my own pain? How can I resist the temptation to become locked in my own sadness?

4. Do I give thanks to God for having had the people I loved for as long as I did? How can past memories help me to grieve *and* feel grateful?

5. Do I believe that God is truly with me as I grieve? Am I convinced that God is with the brokenhearted? What Scripture passages would help to strengthen my faith in this regard? How would the Eucharist help?

6. Am I willing to be compassionate with myself as I mourn my losses? Am I willing to give myself the gift of time?

7. How might my grief transform me? How might it help me to serve others better?

Prayer
FUNERAL PRAYER

God our Father,
Your power brings us to birth,
Your providence guides our lives,
and by Your command we return to dust.

Lord, those who die still live in Your presence,
their lives change but do not end.
I pray in hope for my family,
relatives, and friends,
and for all the dead known to You alone.

In company with Christ,
Who died and now lives,
may they rejoice in Your kingdom,
where all our tears are wiped away.
Unite us together again in one family,
to sing Your praise forever and ever. Amen.[3]

— Chapter 15 —

Old Age

Blessed John Paul II

One type of suffering is inevitable unless we die young: the suffering of old age. No matter what we might do to look and feel young—plastic surgery, diet, exercise, or makeup—eventually we are going to have to address the decline of our physical being. At some point, we will have to face the fact that we cannot do or be at seventy or eighty what we did or were at twenty or thirty.

Although some saints lived to a ripe old age—St. Alfonsus Liguori was in his nineties, for instance—it is only in relatively modern times that living past seventy has become commonplace. This is what the psalmist wrote thousands of years ago:

> The days of our life are seventy years,
>   or perhaps eighty, if we are strong;
> even then their span is only toil and trouble;
>   they are soon gone, and we fly away. (Psalm 90:10)

Learning how to age and come to terms with the concomitant suffering that it entails is a lesson that a famous modern saint has taught us well. Blessed John Paul II was considered young for a pope when he was elected at age fifty-eight. Certainly, he was still very active, hiking, skiing, and traveling around the world. He was vigorous and healthy, breathing new life into the Vatican and the Church. Over the twenty-six years of his papacy, however, we watched as Parkinson's disease exacted its toll, and this once vital man became frail and disabled before our eyes. Finally, as the world held its collective breath, he showed us how to die, and in doing so, he showed us what the Church means by the term "a good death."

No matter what our current age, we can learn vital lessons about how to complete the final chapters of our lives by observing how John Paul II approached his "elderhood" and final passage.

Our Value as a Human Person

The first lesson Blessed John Paul teaches us is that aging is not an evil, despite what our secular culture might have us believe. Aging is simply part of the natural biological process that all living creatures undergo. As a part of that unavoidable course, we will undoubtedly experience some level of suffering, but by accepting the inevitable, we can mitigate the pain and grow old in grace. Our self-worth and value will not be tied up in our appearance or our abilities but in our essential value as a human person. When viewed that way, we will not create additional pain for ourselves by trying to stave off what cannot be put off forever. As John Paul himself observed:

> The sick, the elderly, the handicapped, and the dying teach us that weakness is a creative part of human living, and that suffering can be embraced with no loss of dignity. Without the presence of these people in your midst, you might be tempted to think of health, strength, and power as the only important values to be pursued in life. But the

wisdom of Christ and the power of Christ are to be seen in the weakness of those who share his sufferings. Let us keep the sick and the handicapped at the center of our lives. Let us treasure them and recognize with gratitude the debt we owe them.[1]

A second lesson we can derive from Pope John Paul's example is the importance of keeping our spirits young even as our bodies fail. Too often people grow old mentally and emotionally long before their time on earth is at an end. One of the reasons that young people do not always like to be around the elderly is because older men and women have a tendency to complain, criticize, and denigrate. They become locked in the past instead of being engaged in the present. In doing so, they create pain and isolation for themselves that God never intends. In his 1999 *Letter to the Elderly*, Blessed John Paul made this very point:

We are all familiar with examples of elderly people who remain amazingly youthful and vigorous in spirit. Those coming into contact with them find their words an inspiration and their example a source of comfort. May society use to their full potential those elderly people who . . . are rightly esteemed as "living encyclopedias" of wisdom, guardians of an inestimable treasure of human and spiritual experiences.[2]

By his own example, John Paul showed us how to remain spiritually young even while growing old physically. To be convinced of the importance of remaining active and engaged with the world at large no matter what your age, one has only to watch videos of past World Youth Days. Even when Pope John Paul II appeared before the crowds as a frail old man, he was still able to inspire millions of young men and women at those gatherings as he urged them to seek a deeper meaning for life in Christ and his Church.

YOUNG AT HEART

Just racking up a certain number of years doesn't ensure that we will be inspiring or comforting. That's something we have to work at, but if we take the time and make the effort, we will discover that the rewards are worth it.

In my own life, I am blessed to have friendships with two women who are mentors for learning how to age. One is the widow of a Protestant pastor; the other is the wife of a wealthy businessman. Their lives could not have been more different in terms of possessions, travel, and experiences. Yet as they both approach their eighties, they have shown me that the keys to aging well are to remain active, involved with life, and deeply connected. The pastor's widow has begun to trace her Jewish roots, joining a Messianic Jewish community and counseling young married couples. The businessman's wife has taken up painting, using her newfound talent both to bring beauty into the world and as a means of increasing her philanthropy. What they both do, however, is embrace the now and live fully in the present. They realize the gift of life itself and teach me the power and value of gratitude. I truly find "their words an inspiration and their example a source of comfort," as Pope John Paul said.

A third lesson we can learn from Blessed John Paul about coping with the suffering that comes with aging is that it is acceptable to acknowledge the pain. It hurts to realize that our lives are ending. It's painful to realize that we cannot do what we used to do. It can be sad to acknowledge that there are things we will never get to do. Just admitting the pain can help us, and when we go to God, he will give us what we need to bear it, as John Paul reminds us in his *Letter to the Elderly*:

> When God permits us to suffer because of illness, loneliness, or other reasons associated with old age, he always gives us the grace and strength to unite ourselves with greater love to the sacrifice of his Son and to share ever more fully in his plan of salvation. Let us be convinced of this: he is our Father, a Father rich in love and mercy![3]

And as we have learned from other saints, while we don't have to deny what we are going through, we need not dwell on it either. Constantly fretting about what's happening won't change things. Moreover, if we believe that God will give us what we need when we need it, we will receive it.

Old Age, and Life Itself, Are Blessings

Recognizing that old age has its own blessings is yet another lesson we can learn. Our culture emphasizes the glories of youth, but as John Paul points out:

The teaching and language of the Bible present old age as a "favorable time" for bringing life to its fulfillment and, in God's plan for each person, as a time when everything comes together and enables us better to grasp life's meaning and to attain "wisdom of heart." . . . Old age is the final stage of human maturity and a sign of God's blessing.[4]

As a young man, Pope John Paul II wrote many inspiring words, but in his later works, such as his encyclical on the Eucharist, *Ecclesia de Eucharistia,* he was able to use all the wisdom and experience that he had accumulated over a lifetime. This shows us how wisdom can be one of the blessings that come with age.

Finally, the legacy of John Paul shows us that no matter what pain we might experience as we grow older, life itself is always a blessing. If we give up and fall into depression and self-pity just because we have reached a certain number of years, we create unnecessary suffering, burdens that we need not carry and distress that God does not intend. As John Paul writes to his fellow elderly brothers and sisters:

I encourage each of you to live with serenity the years that the Lord has granted you. . . . Despite the limitations brought on by age, I continue to enjoy life. For this I thank the Lord. It is wonderful to be able to give oneself to the very end for the sake of the Kingdom of God![5]

Live . . . until the very end!

FOR CONSIDERATION

1. What do I fear most about growing old? What blessings do I see in growing older?

2. How am I preparing now for a fruitful and productive old age?

3. Am I locked in the past or do I make an effort to remain connected with the present? In what ways might I be better connected?

4. Am I willing to ask for help as I get older? Am I willing to make changes in my living situation if it helps my children take care of me? If not, what's preventing me?

5. Am I grateful for the gift of life? Why or why not?

6. Do I enjoy my life in spite of any pain or suffering? Am I convinced that God still loves me?

8. How do I respect the aged in my family? Do I do all that I can to make sure that they are being treated with dignity, no matter what their age?

9. Do I feel as if I have accumulated wisdom from my life experiences? If so, do I share them in an encouraging way to those younger than me?

9. Am I willing to give myself "to the very end" for the sake of the kingdom of God?

Prayer
OF BLESSED JOHN PAUL II

With all my heart I seek you;
let me not stray from your commands. . . .
Open my eyes, that I may consider
the wonders of your law.
I am a wayfarer of earth;
hide not your commands from me. . . .
Make me understand the way of your precepts,
and I will meditate on your wondrous deeds. . . .
Your compassion is great, O LORD.

(Psalm 119:10, 18–19, 27, 156)

O God, You are our Creator.
You are good and your mercy knows no bounds.
To you arises the praise of every creature.
O God, You have given us an inner law
by which we must live.
To do Your will is our task.
To follow Your ways is to know peace of heart.
To You we offer our homage.

Guide us on all the paths we travel upon this earth.
Free us from all the evil tendencies
    which lead our hearts away from Your will.
Never allow us to stray from You.
O God, judge of all humankind,
    help us to be included among Your chosen ones
    on the last day.
O God, Author of peace and justice,
    give us true joy and authentic love,
    and a lasting solidarity among peoples.
Give us Your everlasting gifts. Amen![6]

—CHAPTER 16—

LIFE LESSONS ON SUFFERING

When I began writing this book, I was looking for answers to some of my own deepest questions. It's often that way with my writing; I am seeking as much to learn as to teach, to explore as much as to explain. Many times I find that when I reach the end of a book, I have answered the questions that I posed to myself at the beginning—in this case, "Why do we have to suffer?" "What's the point of suffering?" "Does God want us to suffer?"

As I said earlier, much ink has been spilled in search of answers to these questions. And I understand, as the Church teaches, that uniting my suffering with that of Christ's has a salvific effect on creation. But sometimes lofty theological ideas, while inspiring, don't comfort us when we are hurting. When I'm really hurting, with the kind of pain that penetrates body and soul, all I want is for the pain to go away—sooner rather than later.

That's why I was so moved by Pope Benedict XVI's response to the young Japanese girl that I referenced in the first chapter. Her question, asked during a television question-and-answer show on Good Friday 2011, was simple: "Why do I have to suffer?" The pope didn't respond with a complicated treatise on the meaning of suffering or how it relates to salvation. He didn't quote Scripture or even his predecessor, Blessed John Paul II. He simply said:

I also have the same questions: Why is it this way? Why do you have to suffer so much while others live in ease? And we do not have the answers but we know that Jesus suffered as you do, an innocent, and that the true God who is revealed in Jesus is by your side. This seems very important to me, even if we do not have answers, even if we are still sad.[1]

"We do not have the answers." Wow! Even the great theologian Cardinal Joseph Ratzinger, now Pope Benedict XVI, doesn't know why we have to suffer; we just do. It's the same conclusion I've come to after studying the question of suffering as it relates to the saints. We can learn from our suffering and our suffering can help transform us, but why we have to suffer to accomplish these things is simply a mystery. Pope Benedict then goes on to say:

God is by your side and you can be certain that this will help you. One day we will even understand why it was so. At this moment it seems important to me that you know "God loves me" even if it seems like He doesn't know me. No, He loves me, He is by my side, and you can be sure that in the world, in the universe, there are many who are with you, thinking of you, doing what they can for you, to help you.[2]

This, too, reached my heart deep in the aching places. Even when we don't feel loved, we are. Even when we feel alone, we aren't. We do not suffer alone. When my cat was run over, I was stunned by the outpouring of sympathy and understanding from people I barely knew. They wanted me to know that I wasn't alone in my pain, and through their empathy, I wasn't. In some way that I can't fully explain, knowing that others held my pain in their hearts made the pain more bearable.

It's the pope's conclusion that really brought it all home to me:

> And be aware that, one day, I will understand that this suffering was not empty, it wasn't in vain, but behind it was a good plan, a plan of love. It is not chance. Be assured, we are with you, with all the Japanese children who are suffering. We want to help you with our prayers, with our actions, and you can be sure that God will help you. In this sense we pray together so that light may come to you as soon as possible.[3]

These statements by Pope Benedict resonate in my soul: *We don't have a good answer for why we have to suffer, but we can know that suffering isn't useless.* There is a plan for everything that happens to us, including our pain, and we must trust that one day the light will come to us. In the meantime, we must help each other in our suffering.

I have the feeling that Pope Benedict appreciates the practical aspects of dealing with suffering as much as he understands the philosophical reasoning. One reason I say that is because of his prayer intention for December 2010:

> That our personal experience of suffering may be an occasion for better understanding the situation of unease and pain which is the lot of many people who are alone, sick, or aged, and stir us all to give them generous help.

He doesn't ask that we better comprehend how suffering unites us to the redemptive action of Christ, which I'm sure he believes, but instead, he asks that our suffering help us better understand those around us and motivate us to help alleviate their suffering.

So what am I thinking now that this work is drawing to a close? I began by saying that I believe that God does not take pleasure in our pain and suffering. I still believe that. However, I have also come to think that perhaps suffering is necessary, not because it's something God delights in, but because of our own human nature.

I know that I learn in one of two ways: through pleasure and through pain. Learning through pleasure, as in an exciting trip abroad to discover new cultures and people, is exhilarating and fun, but the changes created by the pleasure aren't always long lasting. Much of the time, when the pleasure ends, so do the lessons. In addition, learning through pleasure can have the unwelcome effect of simply wanting more pleasure. This is what happens with drug addicts; they learn that taking drugs brings them gratification, and so they continue to want more and more of that same sensation.

On the other hand, learning through pain tends to be more permanent. How many people do you know who refused to make lasting change in their lives until they scraped the pro-verbial bottom of the barrel? Very often we aren't willing to do what we know should be done until the pain gets great enough. So perhaps that's part of the reason why we have to suffer. Without suffering, we might never be willing to learn the lessons we must learn in life. We have to go through the suffering in order to come into the joy on the other side.

I'd like to leave you with one final quote from Scripture: "For to this you have been called, because Christ also suffered for you, leaving you an example, so that you should follow in his steps" (1 Peter 2:21). I've read this passage many times, almost always in the context of accepting our suffering because Christ suffered as well. However, the story of Jesus does not end on the cross; it ends with a glorious transformation, a resurrection that overcomes the suffering. If we are truly to follow in Jesus' steps, to use his life as an example, then we, too, need to see our suffering not as an end in itself but as a means to our own transformation.

I think the saints would agree.

FOR CONSIDERATION

1. What brings me comfort when I am in pain?

2. How does it make me feel to know that even popes question the reason for suffering?

3. Do I really believe that there is a reason for my pain?

4. How can I turn my own suffering outward to assist others in their suffering?

5. Is there something to be thankful for in the midst of my pain?

6. How can I view my current pain as the means to something greater?

7. Do I learn best through pleasure or pain? Which lessons are the most enduring?

8. What is the greatest lesson I have learned from my suffering thus far?

9. How do I see my sufferings as completing what is lacking in Christ? (Colossians 1:24).

Prayer

OF BLESSED JOHN PAUL II

Together with Mary, Mother of Christ, who stood beneath the Cross, we pause beside all the crosses of contemporary man.

We invoke all the Saints, who down the centuries in a special way shared in the suffering of Christ. We ask them to support us.

And we ask all you who suffer to support us. We ask precisely you who are weak to become a source of strength for the Church and humanity. In the terrible battle between the forces of good and evil, revealed to our eyes by our modern world, may your suffering in union with the Cross of Christ be victorious![4]

PRAYER FOR THOSE WHO SUFFER

For those who suffer, and those who cry this night,
give them repose, Lord; A pause in their burdens.
Let there be minutes where they experience peace, not of
    man but of angels.
Love them, Lord, when others cannot.
Hold them, Lord, when we fail with human arms.
Hear their prayers and give them the ability to hear
you back in whatever language they best understand.
Amen.[5]

ENDNOTES

Introduction

1. "Mother Teresa Dies at 87," by Kenneth J. Cooper, *Washington Post*, September 6, 1977, accessed at http://www.washingtonpost.com/wp-srv/inatl/longterm/teresa/stories/teresa0906.htm.

Chapter 1: Adversity and God's Love

1. "Pope Benedict Speaks on Suffering, Persecution in Historic Q&A," Catholic News Agency, April 22, 2011, accessed at http://www.catholicnewsagency.com/news/in-historic-tv-qa-pope-benedict-speaks-about-suffering-comatose-persons-persecution/.
2. Ibid.

Chapter 2: Physical Pain

1. Letter from St. Padre Pio to Padre Benedetto, Oct. 22, 1918, accessed at http://www.cantius.org/go/organizations/relic_of_st_padre_pio_of_pietrelcina.
2. "The Living Flame of Love," 2.9, taken from *The Collected Works of St. John of the Cross* (Washington, DC ICS Publications), rev. ed., trans. by Kieran Kavanaugh, OCD, and Otilio Rodriguez, OCD, 1991, 661.
3. Letter from St. Padre Pio to Padre Benedetto, Aug. 21, 1918, accessed at http://www.cantius.org/go/organizations/relic_of_st_padre_pio_of_pietrelcina.
4. Quoted on website of the BBC at http://www.bbc.co.uk/religion/religions/christianity/saints/pio.shtml.

5. *Joy in Suffering According to St. Therese of the Child Jesus: A Novena*, by Bishop A. A. Noser, accessed at http://www.religious-vocation.com/redemptive_suffering.html.

6. Kahil Gibran, *The Prophet*, "On Pain," accessed at http://www.4umi.com/gibran/prophet/16.

7. Padre Pio Devotions, accessed at http://www.padrepiodevotions.org/pioprayers.asp.

Chapter 3: Mental Suffering

1. *Mother Teresa: Come Be My Light*, ed. by Brian Kolodiejchuk (New York: Doubleday, 2007), 187.

2. Ibid., 193.

3. "Interview with Mother Teresa," conducted by Edward W. Desmond, *Time* magazine, Dec. 4, 1989, accessed at http://www.servelec.net/mothertheresa.htm.

4. "The Ascent of Mount Carmel," I:13:6, from *The Collected Works of Saint John of the Cross* (Washington, DC: ICS Publications, 1991), 149.

Chapter 4: Physical Disabilities

1. "Alphonsus Liguori Quotes," Brainy Quotes, accessed at http://www.brainyquote.com/quotes/authors/a/alphonsus_liguori.html#ixzz1LQAyHlTh.

2. Search Quotes, accessed at http://www.searchquotes.com/search/Alphonsus_Liguori/2/2.

3. Antonio Tannoja, *The Life of St. Alphonsus Maria de Liguori* (Whitefish, MT: Kessinger Publishing, LLC, 2010), 30.

4. Alphonsus Maria Liguori, *Conformity to God's Will*, 5.4, trans. by Thomas W. Tobin, CSSR, 1952, accessed at http://www.stalphonsusbalt.org/conformity.htm.

5. Website of Queen of Heaven Church, Uniontown, Ohio, accessed at http://www.queenofheavenparish.org /PDFDocuments/Novena_Liguori.pdf.

Chapter 5: Addictions

1. Speech of Pope Benedict XVI, delivered at the Church of the Sacred Heart in Syndey, Australia, on July 18, 2008, during Word Youth Day, accessed at http://www.vatican.va/holy _father/benedict_xvi/speeches/2008/july/documents/hf_ben -xvi_spe_20080718_darlinghurst_en.html.
2. Ibid.
3. "The Last Homily of Father Mychal Judge," Mychal's Message, accessed at http://www.mychalsmessage.org /aboutfrm/homily.htm.
4. Speech of Pope Benedict XVI, delivered at the Church of the Sacred Heart in Sydney, Australia, on July 18, 2008.

Chapter 6: Divorce

1. "Prayers," Catholic Online, accessed at http://www.catholic .org/prayers/prayer.php?p=705.

Chapter 7: Life Choices

1. *The Life and Revelations of St. Margaret of Cortona*, by Fr. Giunta Revegnati, trans. by F. McDonogh Mahony (London: Burns and Oats, 1883), accessed at http://saintsworks.net /forums/index.php?topic=619.0.
2. C.S. Lewis, *The Four Loves* (New York: Harcourt, Brace, 1960), 121.

3. Servant and Steward Blog, "Blessed Damien Quotes," blog entry by Fr. Daren J. Zehnle, February 25, 2009, accessed at http://dzehnle.blogspot.com/2009/02/blessed-damien -quotes.html.

4. Ibid.

5. "Mission Saint of the Month," Missions Office, Archdiocese of Los Angeles, accessed at http://www.missionsla.org /subpages/learn/archivesaint/aprilsaint.html.

Chapter 8: Marital Discord

1. "St. Rita, Our Patron Saint," Website of St. Rita's Parish, West Mifflin, PA, accessed at http://mysite.verizon.net /stritaparish/strita.html.

Chapter 9: Family Matters

1. Butler's Lives of the Saints, accessed at http://www .americancatholic.org/features/saints/saint.aspx?id=1111.

2. *Wings to the Lord* by Jane de Chantal, quoted at "Saint Jeanne de Chantal," Saints.SQPN, accessed at http://saints .sqpn.com/saint-jeanne-de-chantal/.

Chapter 10: Weighty Concerns

1. Centers for Disease Control and Prevention, accessed at http:// www.cdc.gov/nchs/fastats/overwt.htm.

2. *Our Overweight Children: What Parents, Schools, and Communities Can Do to Control the Fatness Epidemic*, Sharron Dalton (Berkeley, CA: University of California Press), 2004, 180.

3. Butler's Lives of the Saints, "St. Francis Borgia," accessed at Bartleby.com, http://www.bartleby.com/210/10/101.html.

4. Ibid.

5. Ibid.

6. Ibid.

7. "The Prayer of Francis Borgia," by John Gavin, SJ, *New Jesuit Review*, 2010, Vo. 1, No. 4, accessed at http://www.newjesuitreview.org/newjesuitreview/Vol._1,_No._4,_A._2.html.

Chapter 11: Prejudice

1. From an article by Sr. Marie Emmanuel, *Immaculata* magazine, Franciscan Friars, Libertyville, Illinois 60048, accessed at http://www.toussaintacademy.org/pierretoussaint.html.

2. Ibid.

3. DisciplesNow.com, accessed at http://www.disciplesnow.com/articles/84/index.html

4. Woodeene Koenig-Bricker, *Prayers of the Saints* (New York, HarperCollins, 1996), 55.

Chapter 12: Temptation to Vice

1. St. Alfonsus Liguori, *The Great Means of Salvation and of Perfection*, chapter 1, accessed at http://www.ourladyswarriors.org/prayer/mustpray.htm#Without%20Prayer%20It%20Is%20Impossible%20to%20Resist.

2. "The Lorica of Gildas," Christian Classics Ethereal Library, accessed at http://www.ccel.org/ccel/pearse/morefathers/files/gildas_08_lorica.htm.

Chapter 13: Financial Stress

1. "Saint of the Day: St. Elizabeth Ann Seton," AmericanCatholic.org, http://www.americancatholic.org /features/saints/saint.aspx?id=1250.
2. "Elizabeth Ann Seton Quotes," accessed at http://www .voicingouropinions.wordpress.com/2010/08/28/saint -elizabeth-ann-seton-quotes/.
3. Ibid.
4 Saints.SQPN.com, accessed at http://saints.sqpn.com /pray0352.htm.

Chapter 14: Grief

1. "A Refusal to Mourn the Death, by Fire, of a Child in London," accessed at Poetry Connection, http://www .poetryconnection.net/poets/Dylan_Thomas/1093.
2. "St. Elizabeth of Hungary," Catholic Encyclopedia, accessed at http://www.newadvent.org/cathen/05389a.htm.
3. Catholic Saints, "Catholic Prayers for Intercession & Assistance," accessed at http://www.catholic-saints.info /catholic-prayers/catholic-funeral-prayer.htm.

Chapter 15: Old Age

1. Address of John Paul II at the Ceremony of the Anointing of the Sick, Southwark's Cathedral, May 28, 1982, accessed at http://www.vatican.va/holy_father/john_paul_ii /speeches/1982/may/documents /hf_jp-ii_spe_19820528_cattedrale-southwark_en.html.

2. *Letter of His Holiness Pope John Paul II to the Elderly*, §12, issued Oct. 1, 1999, accessed at http://www .vatican.va/holy_father/john_paul_ii/letters/documents /hf_jp-ii_let_01101999_elderly_en.html.

3. Ibid, §13.

4. Ibid, §8.

5. Ibid, §17.

6. *The Pope Speaks* 37/4, 1992, 213, accessed at http://www .ewtn.com/johnpaul2/writings/prayers/guidance.htm.

Chapter 16: Life Lessons on Suffering

1. "Pope Benedict Speaks on Suffering, Persecution in Historic Q&A," Catholic News Agency, April 22, 2011.

2. Ibid.

3. Ibid.

4. Apostolic Letter, *Salvific Doloris* (On the Christian Meaning of Human Suffering), 31, issued Feb. 11, 1984, accessed at http://www.vatican.va/holy_father/john_paul_ii /apost_letters/documents/ hf_jp-ii_apl_11021984_salvifici-doloris_en.html.

5. The Sacred Heart, accessed at http://www.thesacredheart .com/psuffer.htm.

the WORD
among us®
The *Spirit* of Catholic Living

This book was published by The Word Among Us. Since 1981, The Word Among Us has been answering the call of the Second Vatican Council to help Catholic laypeople encounter Christ in the Scriptures.

The name of our company comes from the prologue to the Gospel of John and reflects the vision and purpose of all of our publications: to be an instrument of the Spirit, whose desire is to manifest Jesus' presence in and to the children of God. In this way, we hope to contribute to the Church's ongoing mission of proclaiming the gospel to the world so that all people know the love and mercy of our Lord and grow more deeply in their faith as missionary disciples.

Our monthly devotional magazine, *The Word Among Us*, features meditations on the daily and Sunday Mass readings, and currently reaches more than one million Catholics in North America and another half million Catholics in one hundred countries around the world. Our book division, The Word Among Us Press, publishes numerous books, Bible studies, and pamphlets that help Catholics grow in their faith.

To learn more about who we are and what we publish, log on to our website at www.wau.org. There you will find a variety of Catholic resources that will help you grow in your faith.

Embrace His Word, Listen to God . . .

www.wau.org